Out of the box marketing

How to build a super-profitable business

David Abingdon

THOROGOOD

Published by Thorogood Publishing Ltd
10-12 Rivington Street
London EC2A 3DU
Telephone: 020 7749 4748
Fax: 020 7729 6110
Email: info@thorogood.ws
Web: www.thorogood.ws

Books Network International Inc
3 Front Street, Suite 331
Rollinsford, NH 30869, USA

Telephone: +603 749 9171
Fax: +603 749 6155
Email: bizbks@aol.com

A CIP catalogue record for this book is available
from the British Library.

PB: ISBN 1 85418 312 5

Cover and book designed and typeset in
the UK by Driftdesign

Printed in Great Britain by Ashford Colour Press Ltd

Contents

Introduction

Here's a true story...

American astronauts upon first going into space soon discovered that their pens didn't work in zero gravity. So NASA embarked upon a program to invent a writing instrument that would work in outer space. After spending millions of dollars and burning thousands of man hours on research and engineering, they finally developed a 'pump pen' that could write anything, anywhere, at any angle.

Meanwhile, in the secret laboratories behind the Iron Curtain, Soviet Union scientists casually took note of the researches of their American counterparts. They spent almost no time and no money solving this problematic dilemma. They already had the answer, their Cosmonauts used... pencils.

I want you to remember this enlightening little story as you read this book and embark on your goal to become a great marketeer – no matter what it is you want to sell.

Some people spend tens of thousands of dollars and six years in college getting a marketing degree, and maybe an MBA from Harvard or Oxford, only to join the ranks of some corporate giant where they settle down to do 'the same old thing' in the world of marketing and selling.

But you don't need an MBA to become a brilliant marketeer – all you need is this book. I'm not kidding. In these pages you are going to learn what they don't teach at Oxford or Harvard. You're going to learn how to find customers by the thousands, deliver irresistible, high-impact marketing messages to them, and sell them like crazy!

Albert Einstein said: "Sometimes it takes a genius to see the obvious."

Well, I'm no Einstein, but I think you're going to get a similar feeling as you encounter the selling and marketing strategies you'll read about here. It's that – "Why didn't I think of that!" impression you get when you are presented with simple, direct and workable strategies that make things happen for your business.

This is a book on marketing that anyone – a carpenter, a recruitment adviser, a dentist, an insurance agent, a toy retailer, a hairdresser, an undertaker, even a bee keeper – can pick up, apply its ideas and strategies, and make big things happen in terms of business, making money, and having a great time doing it!

This book will tell you how to find droves of customers where you never thought possible, how to tell them exactly what you need to tell them to convert them into paying customers, and how to keep them coming back again and again to buy more.

And you know what? None of the above is important at all if you're not having fun along the way. My goal for you is to not only to become a great marketeer, but to become a person who can get passionate about marketing, about working with people, and making their lives better by selling them fantastic products and services while you earn healthy profits.

NOTE THIS: **all businesses,** no matter what service or product they offer, no matter what they do – from lawyers to tyre retailers and from accountants to grocers – **are in the sales and marketing business**. The purpose of every business is to acquire and retain customers to make money – plain and simple.

More than anything, the sales and marketing business – all business – is the people business. At the end of the day remember that – to treat people right and offer them something that will solve their problems and fulfil their needs and wants – the circle of great business completes itself. You win, the customers win. That's what it's all about.

So let's get started!

BUSINESS PEOPLE WHO SET CLEAR, EXACT, AND HIGHLY DEFINED GOALS HAVE A SPECIFIC TARGET TO AIM FOR, AND TO SHOOT AT.

1

Maximizing your success

Getting to where you really want to be

You would never drive around in your car if you knew it had a dirty fuel filter, or if two of your cylinders weren't working. The car would run like crap, you'd get poor mileage, and you would probably break down now and then. You end up walking two miles in the pouring rain, or worse!

No, you would take the car in for a tune-up at the first sign of trouble to get your engine running at maximum efficiency.

So I ask you, why would you let your business run in a similar state of 'disrepair?' What if your business wasn't running on 'all cylinders?' That is, what if there were a lot of things you could do and change right now that would make your business run more efficiently, and get better 'profit mileage?'

I have no doubt that, no matter what kind of operation you're managing right now, there are a number of easy ways to fine tune it, allowing you to make a lot more money, while not investing a further penny!

What aspects of your business are being underused right now? What assets do you have that are lying fallow, and not pulling all the weight they could be? What's going to waste that shouldn't be? Let's take a look at ways to find your underused assets, and get the most out of them.

Where do you want to be?

Let's start at the beginning. What is your business goal? What is your mission statement? What are your goals for?

- Where you want to be three years from now?
- Where you want to be one year from now?
- Where you want to be by next month?
- What you want to get done this week?
- What you need to get done today?

You have all this written down, don't you? WHAT? YOU DON'T? Then you have a problem! Look: a business that doesn't know exactly what it wants to do or where to go, besides some vague idea like 'sell lots of stuff,' is a business that's already in trouble.

Business people who set clear, exact, and highly defined goals have a specific target to aim for, and to shoot at. If you don't have clear and specific goals, you really have no way to define what you are going to accomplish, and how you plan to get it done. You have no way to plan.

As much as I hate to resort to a cliché: "If you fail to plan, you have a plan to fail!"

Let's say your goal is to make £10,000 profit per month. Okay, exactly what steps do you need to take to get that done, and how much time do you have to sell X numbers of products each day to meet that goal?

If you sell an item with a £100 profit per sale, then you need to make 100 sales a month to meet your goal.

If your conversion rate is 1 in 10 (10%) then you'll need to find 1,000 people in order to convert 100 of them.

So, how much by way of marketing activities – advertising, telephone or sales calls, or direct marketing – do you need to do to attract 1,000 prospects?

By working with specifics you can plan because you know what you have to do to achieve your target – and when you put it all in motion, you can track results, test success or failure, and then make course corrections to change what doesn't work.

So, let's say that in two weeks you're falling short – you've only achieved a third of your goal, say 33 sales... To make 1,000 by the end of the month, you have to implement some new methods, improve your conversion rate or increase your marketing activities.

By knowing what isn't working, you have an excellent idea about where you need to make the changes – and because you have monitored what worked the best, you can re-allocate more resources to the best selling methods.

Can you see what an advantage it is having goals, a specific strategy for meeting them, and a way to test results? You are not working blind. The inefficiencies will reveal themselves before you waste time and money on doing more of them. Better yet, you discover what works, and you concentrate your resources on proven, successful methods, making them even more efficient.

When you test and track results, optimize everything that works, and cut away that which does not pull its own weight, in order for you to maximize results. A £500 ad brought only £200 in sales? Time to change it, or dump it all together! Mike hasn't made a sale all week? Better have a talk with him, or get rid of him! Linda sold

25% more than anyone else? Then you've got a star asset on your hands! Increase her pay, her incentive, and get even more sales from her. Have Linda share her secrets with the less talented sales people. Make her a coach. Maybe she can raise the standard of everybody else?

You see – you are looking at all aspects of your business, bolstering what works and dealing with what doesn't.

YOU MUST WRITE GOALS DOWN! It's just no good to form goals in your head, and then try to achieve them. It simply doesn't work. Writing them down makes them solid and achievable. Then you can check them off your goals as you achieve them, and get solid feedback on how you're doing. The same goes for writing down the specific planning steps you need to accomplish your goals. You must write them down, and then do them.

Defining yourself

Today, more than ever, competition is everywhere. The media is saturated with marketing messages. The average consumer's brain has become like a sponge which has soaked up all the water it can. If the sponge is already full, how can you make it absorb even another drop of your marketing information? It gets tougher every day.

Research suggests that the average consumer is pounded with over 2,000 commercial messages a day! For the average business executive that figure rises to a staggering 3,000! Hard to believe? Think about it, from breakfast to bedtime you are continually bombarded with a vast array of media advertising brands, products and services and everyone of them is vying for your attention: e-mail, spam, billboards, web, radio and TV, magazines and newspapers, personal and business mail, telephone canvassing, cold callers and representatives, shop and vehicle signs – it goes on and on and on.

Unless you're a sad git like me, a lot of this advertising is either ignored, trashed or not interesting enough to be worth your full attention. To most normal people, commercial messages in all their various formats are a boring imposition that clutters up our lives... For the most part, we are just 'not interested'. And that is why most advertising/marketing does not work.

And it just gets worse... We live in a massively over-communicated world where advertisers (businesses, i.e. you) are literally queuing up for the attention of consumers.

So it comes down to this: many business people think in terms of the competition being those businesses that sell similar products or services to a similar market... What's wrong with that? Well think about it... When it comes to the marketing and advertising of your business you are competing for the attention of your target consumer... That's the same consumer that most other businesses – whatever they sell – are trying to get the attention of. In other words you are in competition with everyone else.

For many this is a startling concept and an eye opening reality check. It puts the challenges facing an ambitious business person into context. It also identifies the main marketing problem that most businesses face when it comes to gaining more customers, sales and profits.

But there are solutions...

One way to attack this marketing overkill is to define yourself highly enough, and uniquely enough, so that you clearly stand out from all the other drops in the sponge. So even if your drop of information is in that sponge with all the rest, you can be noticed and recognized over the others.

"INSPIRATION IS ITS OWN MOTIVATION."
JANE ROBERTS

Even if you have ten direct competitors in your geographic market area, you can capture the thunder by working hard to make yourself be seen and known as the best. You need a highly recognizable name and logo that folks can't fail to see and recognize fast. The McDonald's 'golden arches' are a great example. The fast food business has some of the most ferocious competition of any industry. Yet, there are few places in the world where the golden arches aren't instantly associated with a good low-priced burger, even where people can't read a sign in English. The golden arches stand out like no other fast food symbol.

Do you have something that INSTANTLY clicks in the minds of your customer, and makes them associate your product with that logo, symbol, name or whatever? If not, strive to develop it. You don't have to be a behemoth like McDonald's to create something catchy and start using it today. After all, McDonald's started with a single restaurant, too!

Once you have this basic visibility, you need to hammer away at public perception which links your visible image with the high quality, and the best. No matter if you sell insurance, cars, flowers, tropical fish, greeting cards, fertilizer, computers, or beer. Use your advertising cleverly to hammer away at a perception creating effort. Don't slip into mere institutional, image-style advertising. Create ads that sell, but also tailor them to give high visibility to your symbol of quality.

Offer clear-cut solutions in your marketing materials. Create an iron-hard bond between your specific brand and the problems it solves. Customers, more than anything, want solutions to problems. If they equate your brand name with solutions, you're going to reap truly fantastic rewards, and you'll crush your competition, especially if they have not done the homework you are doing right now by reading this!

In addition to your advertising and marketing, every person in your organization who has contact with the public must have a very clear understanding of this vital goal – to build a brand name that is equal to the solution of a problem. All your people, all the time, must be telling everyone they meet that this is what you do – and the better they explain and articulate the details, the more you are going to build your reputation and image as the one to go with.

To make sure this happens, you need to call special meetings and educate your people – and then make sure they understand the mission. Ask your people to repeat back to you what you want them to know in their own words. That way you really know they are 'on message' and ready to get the job done.

Transcend yourself

Take a hard look at your business and ask: "How can I get better? How can I innovate? How can I go beyond where I am now?"

This is tricky, and you have to be careful. That's because, as I say elsewhere in this book, recreating the wheel can be very dangerous. One of the best ways for a new or young business to find early success is to find an existing successful model, and copy it. That way you build on proven techniques already shown to work.

But once you get going, it's very dangerous to stagnate, to always do things the same way, and not expect the rest of the world to pass you buy. You need to innovate and try new things, as long as you do it in a controlled way. Don't change everything at once, putting all your eggs in a new experimental basket. It's better to grow on and around the edges of proven success, and to push the edge forward a little at a time. That means trying a new ad, a new way of reaching customers on your mailing lists, and new ways of delivering your service, a new way to build strategic alliances with others, and much more.

Seek out fresh, innovative people, even if they work way outside your industry. One of the very definitions of creativity is taking two completely unrelated ideas and seeing how they can be melded together to create a new synthesis. For example, do you know who is the biggest seller of children's toys in the world? Think of all the big names in the toy business you can. Well, it's none of them! The biggest toy seller in the world is – (once again) McDonald's restaurants! McDonald's is well known for its Happy Meals and the little toys that go with them. They also frequently conduct special toy promotions tied to major motion picture 'action figures.' Of course, this sounds obvious now, but who was the first person to think about selling toys with food? Someone had to come up with the idea first – after that, all the others struggled to play catch-up.

Look around you? Who or what kind of business might create an all-new strategic alliance with you that will blow the lid off the way anyone has done business before. And don't just look to other businesses. Why not talk to a college physics professor? Or how about a professional actor? Get together with a chemist. What about a Zen monk? All these people deal in their own kind of creativity, and they may have an outlook on the world wholly strange to yours – that's great! You want to 'go where no one has gone before.' Finding a new synthesis that works is difficult, but when it happens, the results can be truly astounding.

Start a mastermind group. This idea was originally credited to Henry Ford by author Napoleon Hill. A mastermind group is a group of people from a wide variety of fields, skills and talents who come together to accomplish goals one business owner would never be able to do using only his own brain power. You can create your own version of a mastermind group with your friends, business associates and anyone else you can lure into the fold, so to speak. Hold monthly brainstorming sessions to see how you, and everyone else, can transcend yourselves, and your way of doing business.

Get passionate, have fun, take a big risk

If you are lukewarm about your business, you'll muddle along with lukewarm results. Only those who are passionate about what they do have the highest chance of success. If you want to maximize your results, you have to be passionate about what you do. If you're not, you have to GET passionate. That means making whatever changes you have to make, including quitting altogether, if necessary, and starting out fresh in that one area of your life where you can feel pulled along effortlessly by sheer inspiration.

Personally, I learnt a long time ago that passion was one, if not *the*, key factor for business success… I once held two jobs. One, the day job, was as a sales manager for a large life insurance company. The other, evenings and weekends, as a jingle writer – writing the music, and sometimes the lyrics, for TV and radio ads. I wrote some good stuff. I thoroughly enjoyed the creative outlet it gave me. I spent most of my day – in the day job – thinking about it. To say I was enthusiastic was an understatement – 'immersed' was the word. I found that I spent most of the money I made in the day job to supply and feed my hunger to be 'around' and 'recognized' in the music scene. I bought the latest recording equipment, keyboards, effects and lots of other stuff.

Then one day, I had a 'moment of truth'. I just wasn't making very much money. The return on my financial and time investment just wasn't happening. So, I got thinking about it… REALLY THINKING ABOUT IT. It just wasn't happening and at the end of the day even if it did, the jingle market wasn't that big and it wasn't exactly full of 'millionaires'. My goals were unlikely to be realized.

Then I had a profound insight: why don't I put all the sweat, enthusiasm, drive and passion into my day job. Give up the hobby and really concentrate my efforts in the sales and insurance field.

I made a decision and I flicked the mental switch. I was ruthless. I sold my gear and got really involved in what made me money. I went from being good at what I did to being one of the best and I received the money and the accolades to prove it.

Now ask yourself: do you need a 'moment of truth'?

It's a funny thing – most people have a hobby, a sport or an interest that they love to pursue. As well as marketing, I run sales training courses. At these sessions I ask for a show of hands from those that have a hobby or a deep interest that consumes some or most of their 'spare' time. As you would expect nearly everyone raises their hand.

Next, I ask for arms to be raised by those who would dearly love, or have a secret longing, to be able to work full- time or dedicate themselves to their hobby. Think about how you would answer? Around 80% raised their hand again. Who wouldn't want to devote their time and life to something that they feel passionate about… whether it is stamp collecting, golf, astronomy or football.

Here's the crux... What if you could make your job your hobby? You would want to work or be involved in it most of your time. You would have the best of all worlds, doing what you love most. That's the knack that the super successful, high performers have acquired. They love what they do because they have reversed the psychology and *made their job their hobby*. They are able to dedicate all of their time to their job because they love it and hobbies are fun. Now it literally becomes a labour of love.

WORK IS NO LONGER WORK – IT IS YOUR LIFE – AND IT'S FUN.

How much do you like what you're doing right now to make money? Do you wake up at three in the morning, and can't sleep because you are just so eager and excited to get going on your work?

If you don't have this kind of passion for what you do, you're wasting your time and your life. Even if your job pays well, hating that job is like living a kind of 'half-life.' You suffer through the work week and live for the weekends.

I urge you to quit the job you have right now, or sell your business if you hate it, and find something you can be passionate about. Forget about the money at first. As the saying goes: "Do what you love and the money will follow."

The great writer Jane Roberts said: "Inspiration is its own motivation." She was right.

In this first chapter, I've only touched on some of the ways anyone can maximize success. A full book on the topic would be easy to write. But any of the suggestions you have just read about – or any one of them – can be all you need to squeeze every bit of profit, passion and power out your business, and your life.

So get the passion going, put yourself at risk, and get moving. Maximizing business success is all about inspiration and motivation. Get them both, and it will be almost impossible for you to fail!

2 High octane marketing

19 ways to supercharge your sales

High Octane 1

Finding your phantom money and making it real

How much do you have to pay for a customer? Are they free? Do customers walk into your business or call or visit your web page for nothing? Have you ever thought about customers this way – as a commodity that you have to buy? Everything else you need to conduct business costs you a specific amount of money. Your office computer cost £1,500. The monthly rent for your office space might be £600. Your electricity bill may run at £95 a month.

But what does each customer cost? The fact is, you have to pay for each customer much like any other commodity that you need to run your daily business. And you have to keep buying them again and again. You only have to buy a new computer every two or three years. Your desk might last 50 years! But not customers! They come, they go. They're an elusive, fluid 'commodity.' Because customers are living, breathing human beings, it's difficult for many entrepreneurs to think of them as a commodity. It's not like you own them once you pay for them to come in. That went out with slavery! So it's easy to forget that each customer you attract is costing you hard cash.

Just look at everything you have to do to find prospects and convert them into customers. Maybe you spend £2,000 a month on advertising. You shell out £1,000 a month on direct mail. You use the telephone, you distribute flyers – it all costs money... You're buying customers! If you spend £5,000 a month on your combined marketing effort, and you bring in 500 customers a month, you're paying £10 a customer. But wait a minute! What if only 300 of those customers actually bought something? After all, they aren't customers until they buy. Before that, they're only prospects, lookers, and time wasters! So if 300 make a purchase, your £5,000 a month for marketing means those 300 customers cost you about £16.66 per customer.

At this point you might say: "Oh come on! Lots of business people calculate how much their customers cost based on what they spend to attract them!"

Is that so? Well, if that's true, then why do so many of those business people make only one sale per customer? If each customer costs hard cash, why don't more entrepreneurs try to squeeze as much business out of them as they can? There may be a lot of reasons, but what it basically gets down to is a mind set. The mindset is this: get customer, sell customer, and look for new customer. Repeat. Get customer, sell customer, and look for new customer. Repeat. Get customer ... okay! You get the picture.

THINK ABOUT CUSTOMERS THIS WAY – AS A COMMODITY THAT YOU HAVE TO BUY

Another reason business people are satisfied with only a single sale to each customer is complacency. Using our example above, if each customer costs the business £16.66, and they sell each of them a £50 product, they're making a nice profit, so what's the problem?

I'll be blunt: the problem is that this is a lacklustre and wasteful way to do business! Even if you're making a profit, settling for a single sale will keep you mired in mediocrity. What separates those who make millions from those who eek out a middle class income? Well, lots of things, and we're going to talk about most of them here, but one of the primary things the super successful marketers thoroughly understand is that making multiple sales to the same customer is a blazing fast way to increase cash flow, and flat out makes a lot more money!

Doesn't it make much more sense to get each bought-and-paid-for customer to buy more than once, and make them buy as many times as you possibly can? If a customer costs £16.66, and you make a £50 sale, that's a profit of about £33.34. But now let's say that after the initial £50 sale, you entice the same customer to buy an extended warranty for an additional £25. Then you sell them a similar, additional product for another £35. So now that customer, for which you paid £16.66 has brought you £110 – and you clean up a £94.34 profit! Best of all, you have not spent a penny to sell that customer a second and third time! Those additional sales are all gravy, as the old saying goes.

Or look at it this way: let's say 500 customers come into your business and rather than making a single sale, you make three sales to all of them. That's virtually the same as having 1,500 customers – and you didn't spend a thing to find and sell those 1,000 additional virtual customers!

In order to make these multiple sales to your customers, you need to be ready to do so while the customer is still in front of you. You must plan to make additional sales even before you open your doors and buy your advertising. If you have a single product to sell, look for a way to incorporate a value added aspect to that product. One of the most popular examples of this are extended warranties offered on electronic items, such as televisions and stereos. Most televisions, radios or computers already come with a warranty included in the original cost, but an extra £25 or £50 extends the warranty for an additional year. Studies show that less than 12% of those who buy the extended warranty ever use it. That means the seller gets to pocket the other 88%! Pure profit! Money for nothing! That's more like it!

You don't have to sell electronics to come up with a value added idea for what you sell. Virtually any product can lead to a second sale of a similar item, or it can be enhanced by a value added attachment. Author James Redfield made millions with his best selling book, *The Celestine Prophecy*. But if you look at the last page of the book, there is an offer for a newsletter which continues to explore the subject the book covered. Price for each newsletter subscription? 45 US dollars! The book itself costs less than £10. Even if only 10 or 15% of the readers opt to subscribe to the newsletter, that's a huge pile of cash since the book sold several million copies. When the reader subscribes to the newsletter, guess what they find in the pages of the newsletter? More offers for more related products, such an audio tape narrated by the author. When they get the audio tape, guess what the author tells them? They can attend a seminar for another fee.

Get the picture? You just keep the "chain reaction" of sales going. To do that, you have to be ready with additional products that fit, match or enhance the original product.

And think about this: what if Redfield's publisher had not included the newsletter offer at the back of the book? In that case, all of those additional sales of millions of dollars would never have materialized! It's kind of spooky when you think about it. It's as if those additional millions are sort of 'phantom money' waiting to materialize—and all they need is the simple idea of making an additional offer tied to the original product. Some marketers call this 'back ending' and others call it 'building an income stream' but it all amounts to the same thing. Look at your product. Can you sense the phantom money hiding behind it? Can you figure out a way to make those ghostly virtual pounds materialize into REAL pounds? Of course you can! AND REMEMBER THIS POINT BECAUSE IT'S CRITICAL: have your additional offer ready to go at the time of the first sale. If you wait two weeks to go back to that customer to make a second sale, that second sale is much less likely to happen.

Try this! Never develop the front end without also building in the back end – and then keep the chain reaction of sales going as long as you can!

High octane 2

Concentrate on the best customers

The invention of the computer has made a certain well-known and explosive marketing strategy work better than ever. Today, all modern retail stores, supermarkets, and many other kinds of businesses, capture specific points of information about each customer sold by entering sales data into a computer. If the computer is programmed to do so, it will automatically record the vital buying behaviour patterns of each customer – patterns which you can analyze and use to make a lot more money while wasting a lot less time.

After a few months of business, you can examine your customer data and find some amazing facts. Certain customers will show up to be your best – that is, they come in more often, they spend more, and they have preferences for specific products. Other customers can be shown to be less valuable – they come in less, spend less, and may also complain more and ask for refunds more often.

Knowing which customers are good and which are not so good is a golden opportunity to dramatically improve your profits, while at the same time, decrease what you spend on marketing.

It's as simple as this: concentrate your advertising and marketing on the good customers, and drop or spend less on the bad customers. You can afford to spend more money on good customers because you already know they are a good investment. You can feel comfortable spending less or nothing at all on bad customers because they don't support your business very well in the first place.

Let's say you are planning a direct mail campaign, and you're using the names of your captured customers for a mailing list. In the 'Old World' you might send a sales letter with discount coupon to every name on the list. Many of those names will be those of customers who are, frankly, more trouble than they are worth. But because you are blind about who's good and who's bad, you have to send to everybody and hope for the best.

But when you have hard data that shows clearly the good customers, you can send your costly marketing materials to them only, and forget the rest.

Also, your computer data can show not just how much your customers spend, but what they like to buy the most. Let's say you own a grocery store. All experienced grocers know that they make little or no money on some items, and make a high profit percentage on other items. But grocers realize they must carry the low-profit items because people still want to buy them, and thus, it brings customers into the store. While they're in the store, the grocer hopes the better paying items will catch the eye of the shopper and they'll buy. Grocers also put certain items on sale, and accept a lower profit, or even a break-even situation, as a way to tease more customers into the store. The hope is they'll buy non-sale items while they're in the store. The problem is that this is a shotgun approach. The grocer has no control. They hope the sales seekers will buy some high-profit items while in the store, but there's no guarantee. Grocers just hate what they call 'cherry pickers.' These are people who watch for sales, and come in only to buy sales items. When grocers concentrate on putting on sales, what they're really doing is catering to lower quality customers! A sale attracts the cherry pickers like flies – but what about the big spenders? Now those are the people they really want!

Well, when you have specific computer data, you can easily tell who comes in to buy the highest profit items the most often. Then, instead of losing cash on sales, you can direct very specific, targeted marketing messages at the big spenders, enticing them to come in and buy more—and to hell with the cherry pickers! The best way to do this is with direct mail. For example, let's say you have iden-tified 300 customers who buy a lot of steaks. It's a high profit product, and now you know who likes them most! All that's left to do is concentrate steak selling messages on frequent buyers with direct mail and you get the best of all worlds – high spending customers buying high profit items!

Also, treating your best customers as 'preferred' customers is an excellent way to reward their buying behaviour. We have long known from basic psychology that when an animal is rewarded for certain behaviour, it will be more likely to repeat that behaviour. That includes humans, and that's the idea here. Reward your best customers by telling them you know they are your best! In your marketing material, you can say something like:

Dear Mrs. Jones

We realize that you are one of our best customers, and we just wanted to take this opportunity to thank you for your continued support of our business. As a gesture of our appreciation, please find enclosed a coupon for a 20% discount on (favourite product here) ...

Furthermore, make sure you let your high quality customer know that they are not only a preferred customer, but that there are many other customers that are not getting the same deal! You want to make them feel exclusive and special. People just love to believe or know that they are privileged in some way. This is one small way you can give them that very feeling.

You can afford to offer high quality customers a discount because you know they'll continue to spend at higher levels, making up your discount in future sales.

No matter what kind of business you are in, and even regardless if you use a computer or not, you can stop wasting time and start making more money by concentrating on your best customers. Why cater to cheapskates with sales, when you can build a 'preferred customer' list with targeted marketing?

One final thing: ask your computer or software dealer for programs which capture and analyze customer data easily and effortlessly. The computer has made concentrating on the best customers more easy than ever. You'd be crazy not to pick up this easy-to-use technology and put it to work for you. The difference it can make in your profit margin can—and will be—truly astounding!

 High octane 3

'Stand on the shoulders of giants!'

Who was the most brilliant man in the history of the world? Well, the best candidate was a slightly nutty Englishman by the name of Isaac Newton. You can name just about anyone else – Einstein, Socrates, Benjamin Franklin, but when it comes to sheer monstrous brain power, Newton had them all beat! (Who says so? Well, the late great astronomer Carl Sagan, for one.)

No, I'm not launching into a lecture on the history of science, here, but I bring up Newton because he quipped one of my favourite quotes. When asked how he accomplished so many great things in science Newton said: "If I have done anything great, it is because I stood on the shoulders of giants."

What a great line!

If you want to accomplish something great in the world of business, I suggest you do the same – stand on the shoulders of giants! If you spend a few weeks reading the works of the great marketing minds of the past few decades, just about all of them will strongly recommend this: find out the lifetime value of your customers.

What is Lifetime Value? Simply this: it is the total cumulative profit a customer can bring you during that customer's buying lifetime, subtracting what you have to spend to capture and sell each of those customers? We've already touched on this in our High Octane Marketing idea No. 1 and No. 2. But it will pay to take a closer look at it because it's important. Indeed, finding out what your customer's lifetime value is, is of extreme importance because it's going to help you become a fantastic marketing success. Best of all, it's really not all that difficult to do.

Let's say a new customer comes into your shop and spends £100. Let's say that customer buys four more times that year, for a total of £450. If you keep that customer coming back for three years, they might spend around £450 per year – that's £1,350. Subtract what you spent on advertising, marketing, overhead on your products, and let's say you get a net profit of £850 for that customer over three years.

If this is the average customer profile, that means each customer is worth £850! Now you have some hard data to work with, and you can use this knowledge to do some wonderful things. If you don't know this kind of information, you're working blind again, just like our example of the grocer in the previous example, who sends out shotgun direct mail packages. Maybe you spend £10,000 a month of advertising and marketing, to get X amount of business, or an X % return on that £10,000.

A blind shotgun approach like this may or may not be sufficient to keep your business going at some kind of profit. But there is almost certainly a huge waste factor in that £10,000 you spend because large chunks of it are hitting prospects that may never buy from you no matter what. Spending money on non-buyers is money burned up in exchange for nothing.

But when you learn how to quantify the exact worth of a particular customer, you begin planning your marketing with your eyes wide open. If you know that a customer will bring you £850, and you spend an average of £50 to sell him or her, that's a net gain of £800. In other words, you have £800 to play with. And this fact leads directly to this strategy: if you spend £50 to get £800, you still have a lot of extra money to attract even more of these kinds of customers.

What this means is that you can decide to spend three or four times more on your marketing tools to attract even more customers. Without fear, without blindness, without flying by the seat of your pants, you can safely spend £100, £150, maybe even £200 or more per customer. Yes, that means you'll make less than £800 per customer net profit—but it also means you are likely to attract twice, three times, maybe even four times as many buyers as you did before! The result is a lot more business, and a lot more money going into your pocket. You know it makes absolute sense to double or triple your advertising budget because the lifetime value of your customers will deliver the profits. The marketer who does not know the value of the customer must blindly buy ads, or send out direct mail, and may quit after spending £5,000 because he or she just has no way to justify spending any more—so they don't! And when they don't, they lose tons of potential business and profits.

Finding the lifetime value of your customer is a simple step-by-step process:

1. Look at your data (you are capturing data, right?) and figure out what your average customer buys and how much they spend.

2. Now, multiply that spend by the average number of times they buy per year. And, multiply that annual spend by the average number of years that they remain your customer.

3. Find out what your net profit is on each customer. That is, subtract the product and associated business costs.

4. What you have left is the money you make – not just on one sale but on all the sales that you make to your customer over the entire lifetime that the customer buys from you. This is extremely useful and powerful information.

5. Now you know the real amount of money that you can afford to spend to acquire more customers because you now know the REAL value of each customer to you.

Notice that you can't do any of this unless you are making sure to capture customer and sales data, and look at what it tells you. It's amazing at how many people don't bother to gather this kind of 'intelligence'. The price such people pay for working blind is often too painful, and I mean painful in the extreme. Failing in business is painful. Getting buried in bad business debt is painful. Having to declare bankruptcy is painful. All of it can be avoided – the very reverse can be had – if you calculate the average monetary worth of your customer, and spend the money to get a lot more of them.

High octane 4

Your unique selling proposition

On any given city block or high street, you may find two, three or four insurance brokers. You might find a couple of dentists. In any part of town, you'll find several car dealers, grocery shops, hardware stores, and more.

What are you selling? No matter what kind of business you're in, you can bet you have competitors. If you have an ad in the *Yellow Pages,* your prospects will find several other dealers to choose from. They're all selling more or less what you're selling.

So why should a prospect buy from you, and not a competitor? What makes you different? If you can't answer this question, you have a problem. The problem is that, in the eyes of buyers, you're just another one of 'the bunch.' Even if you're doing okay business, settling for being just another 'Me Too!' is holding you back. Changing this is a key to making your sales soar to a whole new level.

The way you change, the way you stand out from the pack, is by developing a 'Unique Selling Proposition.' What's that? It's something that you offer or do for your customers that no one else is offering or doing. It's something that makes you clearly better than the others. Interestingly, you may already be different from your competitors. But if your potential customers don't know how or why you're different, they have no reason to choose you over a competitor.

So what you have to do is:

A. Develop a Unique Selling Proposition.

B. Make sure your prospects see it clearly.

Let's look at a couple of examples, and then I'll help you find your own USP.

In a town where there are ten pizza shops, all of which deliver, only one delivers pizza for free. Of course, the free pizza delivery shop probably works the delivery fee into the price of the pizza, but if they advertise loud enough and long enough, people will get the idea they're getting free delivery. Which pizza delivery service will most opt for? One that charges for delivery, or one that delivers free? The answer is obvious. Free delivery is a USP, a Unique Selling Proposition.

Used car dealers compete heavily in the same market for business everywhere. What if one used car dealer offered the option to return the car within 30 days for a complete, no-questions-asked refund if the customer finds the car unsatisfactory for any reason? If none of the car dealers offer the same, that's a USP! Won't a lot of people take advantage of this as a way to get free use of a car for a month? Possibly, but in practice this happens very little. The car dealer with the refund offer will also sell more cars which will make up for any refunds. Also, the car can simply be resold to another customer in the future. There's little to lose, and a lot of business to gain.

So what is your USP? If you don't know, get out a clean sheet of paper and write down every benefit of your product or service. Then examine the same of your competitors. Do you have a clear advantage, a unique offer the others don't? If you can't find one, create one! It can be one of many things: a money-back guarantee, a superior warranty, a free gift along with a purchase, the fastest service in town, and many more. Just make sure you deliver on what you promise! Not delivering destroys your entire USP effort.

Second, you have to work hard at letting people know that you are different. You do that by touting your USP in all your ads. You can also send direct mail to your customer base telling them clearly what your USP is. Tell customers you meet personally why you are unique, and what they won't get if they go to your competitor.

Remember, it's not enough to have a USP. That USP must be clearly communicated to your market. When you successfully develop and communicate a USP, you have given yourself a gigantic advantage over your competitors, and you sell more products.

High octane 5

More on being different – positioning

Developing a USP is one way to stand out from the crowd, but are there more ways to get the job done? Yes! Again, think about the scenario. Three insurance agents on the street all sell similar products at more or less similar prices. So why should people buy from you, and not the guy down the street?

Well, if you position yourself as an expert in your field, people will choose to work with the expert just about every time – even if the expert charges more!

How do you position yourself as an expert in your field? There are several ways. One great way to do it is to write a book and distribute it in your market area. Who will people trust more – the insurance agent who wrote a book on insurance, or the other guys who just sell insurance? You can also make an agreement with a local news-paper to publish a weekly column which discusses the trends in your industry, which also helps prospects get the best deals in your industry. Again, you'll be perceived as the expert. Better yet, your

'DON'T BELIEVE EVERYTHING YOU READ!' THAT'S THE LIMITATION OF EVEN THE BEST PAID ADVERTISING

column will be like having a free ad in the paper every week! You get your name out and your business a mention every time you publish. If the paper pays you for your column, you're getting paid to advertise!

There are many other ways to position yourself as an expert: Make yourself available for public speaking engagements, be a guest (or a regular) on a radio show, or how about publishing your own newsletter and distributing it free to your customers and to new prospect lists?

When you position yourself as an expert, you stand out from the pack, and that can only mean more sales, more profits.

 High octane 6

Endorsements – how to get a flood of new business

When you advertise, even when you have an excellent ad, people are on guard. They know that most businesses will say anything in an ad to get people to come in to buy. So most people read ads with an automatic 'ad filter' working in their minds. That filter constantly says: 'Don't believe everything you read!' That's the limitation of even the best paid advertising.

Is there a way around it? Yes! In fact, there are many. One of the best is the endorsement. When you get another customer, or a well-known individual to endorse your product for nothing, it's like getting a great advertisement that won't trigger the dreaded 'ad filter' in people's minds.

Imagine if a person hears this from a neighbour or friend they have know for years: "You know Bill, if you want to get an excellent deal on a (product) you should go see ABC. I was really pleased with (product) and I got a great price. They're really nice people to deal with!"

What is Bill thinking after he hears this? Well, he's not thinking: "Oh sure he says that, he's getting paid to say it!" That's what Bill thinks when viewing a paid advertisement! But when he hears it from a trusted friend who is getting no kick-back or payment for his endorsement. It's all pure information. Chances are high that if Bill wants that product or service, he will go in and buy.

So the key is to get other people to endorse your product for you. Sometimes it happens spontaneously, but you want to make sure it happens, and happens a lot. How do you get this done? There are several ways. First, you can ask your satisfied customers to recommend you. You can even reward them for the favour. Offer a discount or some kind of freebie for every prospect your customer sends your way. Most of the time, the new prospect will not know, or care, if their friend received an additional incentive to endorse.

Another way is to get a third party to endorse you, such as another non-competing business owner, professional or celebrity. For example, a dentist might send out this letter to his captured customer list:

Dear (Name)

I'm writing to thank you for your loyalty as a patient and to tell you how much I value your business. Because of this I wanted to let you know about an excellent opportunity that may make your life (and dental bills) better. My friend of many years, Rob Jones, is an insurance broker specialising in medical insurance, and he currently promotes a sickness and accident policy which I think is an outstanding deal, and which will also provide you with a great deal of comfort and security in the event that you are unable to work due to illness or injury related reasons.

More to the point, it offers additional ancillary benefits that help towards medical and dental costs. When Rob detailed it to me I knew that it would be something that many of my patients would want. Rob tells me that the plan will give you the confidence and security of knowing you and your family is well cared for in the event that you can't work for health-related reasons. (Something which I hope does not happen to you in a million years!)

Also, I understand Rob is offering the first month free until the 30th of this month. Amazingly, the plan offers you your entire premium payment back in the event you don't use it in 12 years! I can't think of a better deal that comes with so many great benefits.

Feel free to call Rob anytime on 01234 567890 or see him in person. He's located at 123 High Street, Anytown. It won't cost you a penny to talk to him, and I think you'll enjoy hearing about this plan and taking advantages of Rob's special offer.

All the very best,
Jim Dentist

You can bet that a letter like this is going to get a wave of business heading towards Rob Jones, insurance broker! An endorsement that's sincere and compelling is simply going to get the job done.

An important thing to note: a good endorsement should not be lukewarm or basic or matter-of-fact. The best endorsements are enthusiastic, warm and personal. You certainly have associates who you can contact right now to arrange an endorsement. Offer to do them a favour if they do you a favour. You can offer access to your customer list in exchange for their help.

The endorsement does not have to come from anybody famous or a celebrity, although that really would be a good thing. The problem with the famous, however, is that they're difficult to contact, expensive and even more difficult to get an endorsement agreement from. Luckily, you don't need them! You'll have all the business you can handle if you get local, respected ordinary people to give you a pitch.

 High octane 7

Direct mail

If the Devil himself visited me this afternoon, and told me that I would only be allowed to use one marketing tool for the rest of my life as punishment for my evil ways – I would probably choose direct mail.

What makes direct mail so great? It's simply a terrific way to go directly to your prospect, get in their faces and make them one hell (pardon the pun) of a great offer they can't refuse. Better yet, you can reach thousands of people fast, and for less cost than just about any other kind of marketing tool. But wait, you say! Isn't direct mail risky? Don't most people consider mailed marketing pieces junk mail? And don't 95% or more of those same people toss out 'junk mail' without so much as opening it?

All true, all true but consider this: even if 95% of everybody tosses your direct mail piece, and then only half of those end up buying, you're still going to make an incredible amount of money. With just a 2 or 3 percent converting to successful sales, direct mail will not only pay for itself, but earn you a terrific profit. Let's look at some numbers:

You mail 5,000 pieces which may cost you about 50 pence each, paying for postage, paper and envelopes. That's £2,500.

You are selling a £100 item.

You get a 2 % successful response rate. 2% of 5,000 is 100.

How much is 100 x 100? That's £10,000! You just spent £2,500 to gross £10,000!

Let's say your £100 product cost you £35. That's £3,500. Add that to your mailing costs, £2,500, and you get £6,000. Subtract another £1,000 (10% for miscellaneous expenses) and you get £7,000. So you still have £3,000 left over in pure profit.

By now, I hope you're starting to see the magic of direct mail. With a mere 2% success rate, you're making fast cash. But if you do it right, it's not unusual to sometimes get a 5, 10 or even 20% success rate. When that happens, you have money raining down on you like an April shower.

A few years ago, a book was released called, *How to Fight Cancer and Win*. The publisher test marketed a direct mail piece and was delighted to get a nearly a 20% response rate. Based on that success, he sent out 50,000 direct mail pieces plugging the book. His response rate for those 50,000 was an incredible 24%, or about 12,000 sales. After all expenses, he was clearing about £8 per book. His profit: £96,000. Another mailing of 100,000 was almost as successful, a 22% successful response rate. That's 22,000 sales at £8 for a profit of £176,000.

Not bad.

Direct mail costs far less than advertising, cold calling, telemarketing, live selling door-to-door, and all the rest. At the same time, it brings in far more money that all of the above.

The cautions I have for you about direct mail are these:

- Not just anyone can create direct mail sales materials, such as sales letters and brochures that work. A poorly crafted sales letter may easily fail to get a single response, even if you mail out thousands of them! Writing direct mail sales copy is a fairly high and refined art. Entire books have been written on the hows and whys of direct sales copy writing. It can be that complex!

- There are other pitfalls, as well. A major factor is the mailing list you choose to send your direct mail. If you have a bad list, you're going to get a terrible response, even if you have a fantastic sales letter with a great offer.

STRIVE CONSTANTLY TO FIND OR CREATE NEWS ANGLES ABOUT YOUR BUSINESS, PRODUCT OR SERVICE

Because direct mail is such an important tool, we'll revisit the topic later in this book. But for now, we urge you to start looking into your own direct mail campaign. Do your homework first, and then get mailing. There's a lot of money out there waiting to come flying back into your mailbox!

High octane 8

Ads that you can get for free and that out-pull by 2,000%!

Remember in High Octane 6 when I said that people come equipped with an 'ad filter' pre-installed in their brains? Well, what if you could get an advertisement that by-passes the 'ad filter,' and better yet, what if that advertisement cost you absolutely nothing? Sound like a dream? Just too good to be true? Wrong and wrong.

You can get free advertising that can be 2,000% more effective than advertising you have to pay for. Free advertising does not look like advertising because it basically isn't advertising! So what is it? It's publicity! It's a story about your business or product in a local or major media outlet that says good things about your product. These stories are written by journalists working for newspaper, radio and TV. Why would they do that? They'll do it if they find something newsworthy about you, your business or your product. What they absolutely will not do is give you free ink or air time if they find no news value related to you or your product.

So I recommend you take the advice the American billionaire media magnate William Randolph Hearst, who said: "If there is no news, we'll make some!" Hearst was in the business of selling newspapers, so hot news stories are what he thrived on. You need to come up with a newsworthy angle for your business, product or service to make it slip past the media gatekeepers to get some free ink or air time.

How do you do that? You have to be creative, and you have to understand what makes news and then make some news happen. You do that by doing something newsworthy. Here's an example: a hotel decided to adopt about 20 cats from a local animal shelter. They kept most of the cats in the lobby. When guests arrived for a room, they were given the option of having a 'complimentary cat' in their room if they wanted one – a very unusual angle.

The result? The story was big news. The story had legs – it was run again and again in thousands of newspaper, TV news programs, and even radio. The story made several national news programs. Better yet, the story was so interesting, it was covered every couple of years by somebody. That's literally millions of pounds in 100% free ink!

Now here's the kicker: free publicity like this works far better than ads because when people confront the story, they are aware that what they are reading is not an ad, but an objective news story. Thus, their internal 'ad filter' is turned off. The positive message about your product penetrates directly into the prospect's mind, uninhibited by anything. The result can be a massive influx of new business.

Another way to get free ink is to issue press releases about your business or product – but again, these must have a rock-solid news angle, and must never be an obvious attempt to get free publicity. Editors hate nothing more than attempts to be used in this way.

Strive constantly to find or create news angles about your business, product or service. The pay back can be absolutely astronomical, and I mean really, really BIG!

High octane 9

Whatever you do, don't waste time!

Why do you think banks traditionally placed clocks outside their buildings? Because they know that time is money. In fact, it's with banks that this whole idea of calculating interest rates – based on time – got started. If you have a loan, it's that inevitable, unstoppable ticking of the clock which is determining how much money you owe in interest payments.

If you really want to look into this more deeply, read up on the history of capitalism and banking. You'll be amazed. Our entire monetary system rests upon a modern concept of time, which was given to us by astronomers, such as Copernicus, Galileo and Newton. Indeed, it is Sir Isaac Newton's 'clockwork universe' that has shaped our modern conception that time = money, perhaps more than anything else.

Ever wonder why we say: "How do you plan to SPEND your time?" It's because time and money are intimately tied to each other.

Okay, had enough of the history lesson? Want me to get to the point? The point is that the statement 'time is money' is far more than a cliché. It's a basic reality because of the fundamental way we do things.

And I can't make this statement strongly enough: NOTHING IS MORE VALUABLE THAN YOUR TIME! At the start of each new day, you are issued a fresh 24 hours – that's 1,400 minutes and 86,400 seconds! If you think of each of those hours minutes and seconds as having a monetary value – and they do – every one you waste is money lost forever.

You must start paying attention to your time each day, and how you spend it. How much actual time do you commit to making money with your business? You don't know if you don't pay attention. If you start keeping a daily log of how much time you actually spend on money making activities, you may be in for a surprise. What about all that time spent chatting around the coffee machine? It can be nice, but it earns you nothing. Do you waste time with people? Most do. If you decide to spend 15 minutes shooting the breeze about the World Cup, even if it's with a client, that time is lost money. And we all know people that are what I call 'dumpers.' These are people who call you up or visit personally and steal 20 or 30 minutes just telling you about their problems. It's great for them because they feel better after unloading on you – at the expense of your precious time. But you get nothing, except for the reputation of being a 'good listener.'

There's nothing especially wrong with that, but when it's time to conduct business, then you should be doing business. I suggest that no less than 90% of your day be focused on making money, and making things happen for your business.

The biggest reasons people waste time are because:

A. They have not internalized and do not remain conscious of the fact that time is money.

B. They simply aren't paying attention.

Play a mental game with yourself, starting at minute one of your next day. Every 15 minutes or so, stop and ask yourself: "Is what I am doing right now moving me forward toward my earning goals?" Do it every 15 minutes. Set an alarm clock if you have to. A wrist watch with a timer on it that beeps is great for this. The idea is to shake up your conscious and unconscious mind. Wake yourself up as to how you're spending your time! Put yourself on notice: "I will stop wasting time!" The thing about wasting time is that it's insidious. It creeps up on us while we're not paying attention. Before we know it, days, weeks and months are lost in non-productive activity.

But once you get aware of this – once you 'awaken' to the idea that every moment counts – you'll stop wasting time, and you'll start getting things done twice as fast, three times as fast, or even faster. When that happens, I promise you that you'll notice a magical effect. You'll start getting a lot more done and – again this will seem magical – you'll start making a lot more money!

Best of all, paying attention to time during work actually frees up MORE time to spend with family, loved ones and your favourite non-work activities. So stop wasting time. Time is truly money. Ultimately, you've only been allotted a certain amount of time on this planet. Why waste it?

High octane 10

Remove the risk, and they'll buy

All buyers have a half-dozen reasons or more to not buy: don't need it, costs too much, not sure if it's a good deal, unsure about quality, and so on.

The savvy business person knows that for every one of these reasons they knock down, they remove a roadblock to a potential sale. If you want to get people buying, you have to make it easy for them to buy by removing doubt, risk and reasons not to buy.

One of the best ways to do that is with a rock-solid money-back guarantee. It's incredible how many business people are unwilling to offer a money-back guarantee. They immediately think of the negative: "I'll have to refund money that's in my hand now!" But this is short-sighted thinking.

If you offer a money-back guarantee, what you are telling the prospect is: "I am so convinced you'll like my product, I'm willing to stand behind it with a money-back guarantee." And the prospects thinks: "Hey! I risk nothing. If I buy and don't like the product, I get my money back. So why not buy now?"

And really, why shouldn't you stand behind your product? If you're not willing to stand behind your product, why should the customer assume all the risk by buying from you? You owe it to your customers, and to yourself, to back up your products and service. Those not willing to guarantee their work may be wittingly or unwittingly operating under the 'a sucker is born every minute' philosophy. They think there will always be a new customer somewhere out there who hasn't heard anything negative about them.

And there'll always be more after that. But this is a stupid way to do business. Experienced marketers know that the REAL MONEY is made on repeat sales, repeat business, and 80 to 90% of new business comes from endorsements or referrals from satisfied customers! Also, constantly having to find new customers is expensive. As you read in High Octane 1: Each new customer costs you money to find and sell, but each repeat sale to a captured customer is free.

When you use risk reversal, it's common to see a doubling, tripling or even greater boost to sales – without spending an additional penny for more marketing! Yes, there will be some returns, but the volume will almost always be in your favour – if you're delivering a high quality product that does what you promise it will do.

But even if you do get returns and complaints, that's not necessarily a bad thing. It's an opportunity to find out what your weaknesses are, and how you can eliminate them. If you can fix the problem, your returns will shrink even further, and you keep more profit. You also build your reputation as a high quality dealer. When that happens, even more sales flow in! Are you starting to see how this all works together?

The stronger you make your guarantee, the better the result. A full refund for return of the product within 30 days is very good. Even better is allowing the item free for 30 days, with payment due after that period, or no payment necessary when the product is returned. But you can still go even further! For example, offer a guarantee that says the product must pay for itself two, three or five times over, or the customer's money is returned.

In the second scenario – no payment for 30 days – notice that you also remove a second reason not to buy. The customer can get your product even if they are short of cash today. Buy now, pay later is still one of the best sales boosters ever invented, and there's no reason why you shouldn't start trying it today.

Is all this just too much risk for you? I urge you to reconsider. The stronger the risk reversal strategy, the more your sales explode, the more you build your reputation as a high quality company that deals fairly with each and every customer. The more reasons you remove for a prospect to buy, the more they will buy. In the long run, and even in the short run, you make more sales and more money.

High octane 11

Want an ad that's 500% more effective? Then test!

This has happened so many times it's almost legendary, yet for some unknown reason, very few entrepreneurs learn from it. What am I talking about? This: a business person decides to change just a word, or two, in an ad's headline, and suddenly the sales increase by 500%, and sometimes even more. Note that nothing else in the ad changed: same product, same price, same deal all around. Yet a slight alteration in the headline multiplies its effectiveness by dozens of times.

How and why does that happen? What makes the big difference? The vexing thing about advertising is that, most of the time, nobody know what's going to work, or how it works – and they don't know why it works when it does! It's true! There's always an element of risk and gamble in any advertising attempt. The reason for this is that advertising is not an exact science, and the reason for that is the natural unpredictability of the interaction of many variables in an ad.

For an ad to be a great ad, a lot of things have to come together and click. The ad needs to be seen by the right market – a market that is ready for what the seller is offering. The medium must be the correct one. (Who's going to buy a cookbook from the back of a car magazine?) The price has to be attractive. The timing is important – few people want to buy a lawn mower in the dead of winter, to make a somewhat obvious example. There must be a need or desire for the product. The headline must grab attention and make a promise that is believable. And more.

Some of these variables are obvious, such as choosing the right advertising vehicle for what you're selling. Indeed, perhaps 80% of everything in an ad is under your control – but it's that mysterious 20% that creates problems – or spells opportunity. Even the most successful, experienced ad writers only get it right about 70% of the time, and then, many successful ads are not as successful as they could be. There's just no hard mathematical or scientific formula that can guarantee a great ad every time.

Thus, much of the time the only way to improve an ad is to test it. When the results of the first ad come in, you get a baseline for the ad's effectiveness. If the results are spectacular and profitable from the first run, you've got a winner, and there's little reason to change things until the ad stops working, though you might continue to test to make it even better.

But many times changing the wording of a headline, or altering the offer made in the ad's body copy, can completely transform an ad. Most often, why the change has made the ad better remains a mystery. But in advertising, it's not always important to know WHAT works as long as it DOES work!

So you should be testing your ads, and testing them often. Play with all the variables. Try different headlines. Try a different price or offer. Emphasize a different benefit if your product has more than one benefit to talk about. (Be careful: you usually can only make one point in an ad. That means plugging one specific benefit.) How about your ad's illustration? Is it pulling its own weight? That is, does your ad's illustration help by catching the eye of the reader, or is it merely 'filler.' Every square centimetre of an ad must do its job, or you weaken the ad.

When testing an ad you must pay for an ad several times, just to see which version works best. Yes, that costs money. But when you hit on an ad that pulls response with a vengeance, you'll make so much money with that ad – and you'll likely continue to make money with it far into the future – all your testing will have been more than worth it. Indeed, one excellent ad may be all you need to get incredibly rich!

So test, test, test. It's the key to finding your way to an ad that not only pays for itself, but which can bring in spectacular amounts of money. Testing can mean the difference between outright failure and total success. It's that important!

SOME FINAL TIPS: always be watchful and observant. Start an ad file. Clip and save the best ads you find and study them. Use them, adapt the best of them for your own business. The same goes for sales letters. You probably already get a half dozen a week as 'junk mail.' Save them and dissect them. Call the company who sent them to you to ask how well the letter worked. Listen to radio ad and observe television ads. If you see a print ad or hear a radio ads that has been running for three years straight, you can bet that ad is working for the seller. Why else would they keep buying the same ad for three years if it wasn't working?

Sometimes, it's as easy as looking out into the market place to find marketing gems gleaming everywhere. All you have to do is pick them up and make them work for you.

High octane 12

What you can learn from a farmer

Ask a farmer how the harvest is going, and he'll cut right to the vital statistics: "I'm grossing £400 an acre. My cost (for fuel, fertilizer, machinery etc.) is £375 an acre. So I'm making £25 an acre. I've got 2,000 acres, so I should net £50,000 out of this harvest, if the price holds."

What about a clothing store, a car dealer, an accountant, or a pizza delivery service? Why shouldn't they look at their 'acreage' and make a similar determination?

A business' 'acreage' is their existing market area. They can measure 'yield' by how much money they make in their existing market area. If you take some time to find out what your 'yield per acre' is, you can find out how well you're doing, and then come up with a strategy to do even better.

You probably already know where most of your business comes from, and the geographical area your prospects live within. For any business in a large town or city, the prime acreage is most likely an area within a four to eight mile radius of the physical location of the business. You can safely calculate that some 80 to 90% of your customers live in that circle.

Now find the total number of people who live in your business radius. You can get such information from the postal services or the Internet. Let's say you find out that there are 20,000 people on your 'plantation.' Next you look at your customer list. You find that you have about 1,500 steady customers.

This reveals something interesting: 1,500 is 7½% of 20,000. So you know your "yield per acre" is 7½%. You have 7½% of the market captured. Now you have a clear way to set a new goal! How do you bump up your acreage yield to 15%, 20%, or more?

Knowing precisely where you stand gives you a baseline from which to work, and a clear idea about setting a new goal. As we know from the science of goal setting behaviour, when you have a clear, specific goal to shoot for, you hit the mark more often. If you have fuzzy goals, you get fuzzy results.

Now, there are two basic ways to improve your yield per acre:

A. You can increase your 'market share' by getting more of those 20,000 to come in and be your customers.

B. You can increase your 'wallet share' by getting your captured 7½% to buy more. If you double your sales to your captured market, it's like boosting your yield per acre to 50%!

Take a hard look at what you are doing right now to get your usual 7½% yield. A lot might be simply walk-in business – passers-by who notice your business and drop in. Maybe you advertise in the local paper. Find out exactly how much that contributes to your yield. In short, look at all your marketing tools and then think about which ones you aren't using. If you apply new and additional marketing tools, you may be able to bump up your yield per acre.

MAKE A GREAT OFFER OR OFFER SOMETHING FREE – EVEN IF IT'S ONLY A CUP OF COFFEE, OR A FREE CONSULTATION

You can start small or big. Why not send a postcard with a high impact sales message on it, including an irresistible offer, and send it to all 20,000 people on your plantation? It's amazing how many small businesses never pick up the high octane power of direct mail and put it to work for them. Direct mail is not only for the 'mail order' companies!

How about hiring a couple of bored teenagers to go to every household or business within your acreage and put a leaflet through each letter or mail box? On the leaflet is a can't-resist offer to come into your store or place of business! Give them a reason to come in. Make a great offer or offer something free – even if it's only a cup of coffee, or a free consultation.

If you have determined that you are currently squeezing maximum productivity out of your current acreage, why not start looking outside your plantation?

Think the way a farmer does. A farmer does all he can to achieve maximum yield on his limited number of acres. He might try new fertilizers, better pest control, new seed varieties – all can boost yield per acre. What can you do to squeeze more out of your acreage? You'll have a great time finding out!

High octane 13

Looking for your market?
Go where they go!

In the previous example, we talked about going to your market and ferreting out more customers from the geographic area of your market.

It's a great idea, and you'll get more customers, but what about 'high quality' customers? What am I talking about? A high quality customer is someone who has a very strong need for your product. They hardly need to be sold to because they already want what you have. To find these valuable people, you should dabble in what is generally known as 'target marketing.' Target marketing is different from seeking anybody and everybody to buy from you. It's about concentrating your efforts on a carefully selected group.

So where do you find them? First, identify who your prime prospect is. What do they do? Where do they live? Where do they go when they gather in groups? If your target market candidates are a specific group, that means they all have something in common. You can reach these people by understanding what they have in common because these common traits tend to bring them together.

For example, let's say you deal in products that would interest people who manage or own timber yards. Thus, you should go where timber dealers go. Timber dealers have professional organizations. They get together to discuss the lumber business. You should go to their meeting. Get invited to speak at their next convention. Work the crowd. Talk to timber dealers to see what they're thinking, and what their needs are. Once you get to know timber dealers better, you can develop a relationship with a few of them.

The next time you make a sale to one of your new timber dealer friends, you can ask them to refer you to another timber dealer. You could also bring along a list of other timber dealers and ask your friend, "Mike, which of these other lumber men on this list do you know, and which might be interested in talking to me?" When you get to the next guy, you show him the list and ask for another lead. You can also advertise in their professional trade journals. You'll be reaching a highly focused, tight target market. If your product is what they need, you can't miss!

Get as specific as possible. For example, if you're looking for accountants, maybe what you really want is a tax accountant, or an accountant who specializes in bankruptcy. It can make a huge difference. You can stop wasting time on poorly qualified prospects and concentrate your time and energy on the very best, most highly qualified markets.

I've already mentioned trade publications. Just think of a trade or profession, and you can bet there's a publication serving them. Nurses, dairy farmers, truck drivers, architects. They all have at least one, and mostly likely two or three specialized publications providing information about that industry. When you advertise in these, you have no doubt about who will see your ad. You don't waste money on shotgun approach ads in more general publications. Even a popular magazine or newspaper with sky-high circulation figures can pull fewer customers than a very small circulation publication serving a tightly focused audience.

TRY TARGET MARKETING! YOU CAN'T AFFORD NOT TO!

High octane 14

Your customer has no money?
No problem!

What if you're in front of a customer and they say they would love to buy your product, but they just don't have the money right now? Is that a certain sale killer? Not if you can look beyond the present moment. Not if you want to make this person a customer today, and a repeat customer tomorrow! If you're selling a water purifier, and you're certain your customer wants it but has no money, you can say: "No problem! We'll install the water purifier today, and you pay nothing. We'll come back next week and you can make a £50 payment. We'll stop back once a month to see how the system is working for you, and you can make another payment then. If you don't like it, we'll just remove it and you pay nothing."

Actually, this is a true story. A salesman was selling a water purifier door to door in a large Canadian city. He was tired of getting turned down for the sale for the same old reason – no money. So he offered to install the system free, and set up an easy payment plan for his $400 item. The result? He sold more water systems in the next month than he had in the previous six months! And he never looked back. Very few reneged on their payments or the system, and he made a lot of sales. Better yet, when he went back to collect and see how they liked the system, he sold additional products, such as filter replacements.

Just look at the insurance companies. Very few people like taking out insurance policies – never mind paying for them. Many years ago the insurance companies made a quantum leap in the way they did business… Why not let people pay for their house, car, life or accident insurance by monthly instalments instead of the annual premiums they were currently demanding? Suddenly, insurance became affordable to the masses. With a bit more marketing they also made it essential.

The 'no money' road block is one of the most common reasons not to buy – and also one of the most easy to overcome. Offer a payment plan. Let them charge it. Extend credit. Take credit cards if you don't do so already. Let them try it free for 30 days.

Why don't more business people do this? Probably because they see only the risk and not the gain. They think: 'I'll pay later may mean I'll never get paid at all!' But time after time, hundreds of businesses have multiplied their sales and client bases by enormous amounts with just such a strategy. It's a proven technique. Accept it. Try it. Do it!

 High octane 15

Go ahead – break it!

One of the top insurance salesmen in the world is Sid Friedman who lives near Philadelphia in the U.S. Friedman is a legend in the world of selling. One of his most well-known quotes when it comes to the selling business is: "If it ain't broke, break it."

And Sol Price, the founder of the FedMart discount chain and Price Club warehouse stores, once told a friend of mine: "I've always believed that if you just sit on your backside and say, 'If it ain't broke, don't fix it,' that somebody is going to come along and fix it for you."

CAN YOU BE THE FIRST TO OFFER A TERRIFIC NEW SPIN ON THE SAME OLD BUSINESS?

What do these two sales superstars mean? A couple of things. For one, it's not enough to do just what everyone else is doing. It's also not enough for you to keep doing the same things you are already doing, even if business is doing okay right now. Sooner or later, a competitor is going to shake up your world and do things differently and maybe a lot better. Before you know it, your customers are flowing to that competitor, and then you have to scramble to play 'catch up'. Playing catch up is no fun. That's desperation and a reactionary way of doing business, not a proactive strategy you have planned and shaped to command maximum success. You should always strive to lead, and let others play catch up with you!

In the world of business, you must be prepared to change everything from the ground up. If you don't, as Mr. Price says, someone else will – and you'll be in a hole!

But are we talking about here, specifically? It's what experienced business people call 'differentiating.' Differentiating can be cosmetic, or fundamental. An example of a cosmetic differentiation is to change the package on the same old product. Sometimes, in business, perception is everything.

Differentiation can also be more fundamental, such as a change in the product itself. How many times have you seen 'new and improved' on a familiar product? Laundry soap companies change the chemistry of their soap to make it more effective. Car companies strive to make engineering improvements on their cars every year. Do you remember the days when cars didn't have air conditioning, power steering, anti-lock brakes, and quadraphonic stereo sound? Well, years of fundamental differentiating has transformed the automobile from a 'horseless carriage' to a rolling luxury hotel room, some even with television and cooking utilities! It's all because of the constant drive of differentiation.

But sometimes differentiation is a disaster. Back in the mid-1980s, the mighty Coca-Cola company decided to change its formula for the best selling soft drink of all time – Coke! They made it sweeter, and to taste more like it's arch rival, Pepsi. The result was earth shattering! Coke drinkers raised such a mighty outcry, Coke quickly reversed itself and began reissuing the original formula as Coke Classic. Eventually, they dumped the 'New Coke' formula altogether.

The moral of the story is: you must strive to differentiate, but realize that the process comes with some risk. Yet, you must take this risk and push forward. It's much more dangerous to stay static and do nothing.

Look at your product or service. What can you do today to differentiate and make your customers take a new look at you? Here are some examples:

1. A photographic shop's primary business was taking portraits of people. Then the owners got the idea to take 'glamour shots.' What's that? They hired hair stylists and make-up artists to transform their clients to make them look like movie stars. They also provided glamorous clothing, and even jewellery for one-time use. Then they took a 'glamour shot.' The effect was to literally transform the 'ordinary' look of the client, and make them look over-the-top fantastic! No other studio in town was doing the same thing – but you can bet the others hustled to catch up. By the time they did, the first photographer to do

glamour shots cleaned up on the first surge of business, and also captured a significant share of the market.

2. When most petrol stations switched over to the self-service concept, one service station in a town of 'me too!' operators decided to differentiate. When a car pulled up, an attendant rushed out and started filling the petrol and washing the windows. Before the customer could say anything, the attendant would say: "Don't worry. You pay no extra for full service here!" Word spread fast and this service station got a leg up on the competition.

3. Did you know there was a time when no pizza restaurants delivered? It's hard to believe, but when a company called Dominos Pizza started delivering, it changed the entire industry! All the others had to scramble to catch up!

Can you be the first to offer a terrific new spin on the same old business? If you do, you'll capture the first wave of an entire trend, and those that ride the wave first and fastest, enjoy the greatest success! If you don't look for ways to make positive changes, you risk going static and losing out to someone else who has the courage to 'break what isn't broken!'

High octane 16

They go away quietly

A friend of mine recently told me this story

"I bought a new computer – the fourth unit I had purchased from the same dealer. In the past three years, I had spent about £10,000 there. Well, I get home and set up the new computer and love it, but then the screen freezes. I turn it off, and turn it on again, and it freezes again. So I call up the dealer to ask what's wrong, thinking it's some minor glitch that can be cleared up in a few seconds. It usually is. When I get the dealer sales assistant on the phone I explain my problem and ask what I should do. The guy says, 'Do you have a service contract with us?'

'No,' I say, 'but I'm sure this is just a minor problem. Can I talk to your tech person for a minute?'

He says, 'Well, if you don't have a service contract with us, we need to charge you £25 for each question you have for our technical expert.'

I say, 'Oh I see,' and I hang up. Then I think to myself: 'You know, I've spent about ten grand there, but I sure as hell am going to spend my next ten grand somewhere else!'

That computer dealer has just lost a customer, but he may not know it yet. Studies show that's what happens when you do something to make a customer angry. Most often, they don't complain, they just go away – quietly. They go to your competitors.

"BE EVERYWHERE, DO EVERYTHING, AND NEVER FAIL TO ASTONISH YOUR CUSTOMERS."
MARGARET GETCHELL OF MACY'S DEPARTMENT STORE

Furthermore, according to customer behaviour expert Michael LeBeouff, when a customer has a bad experience with a seller, they tell an average of 20 other people about their painful experience. On the other hand, satisfied customers very often tell nobody else, and sometimes, just two or three other people about a good experience. There's just something about getting insulted, ripped off, or cheated that makes a person want to get the experience off his or her chest by telling it to other people. But if you have a happy experience, you tend to just get on with life.

When you consider that positive word-of-mouth advertising – referrals and endorsements – accounts for up to 90% of repeat business for most companies, it makes it all the more clear how devastating the opposite – this negative word-of-mouth 'anti-advertising' – can be. Whole armies of customers go away and potential customers don't come in after hearing about how a particular business treated a pal.

One of the very best ways to increase those all-important repeat sales is to resolve customer problems in their favour, even if doing so costs you some money or profit. What you lose in the short-term comes back at you many times over in repeat sales from customers who view you as an honest dealer who cares about customers.

When in business, you should not be in the business of making sales. You should be in the business of creating customers, and happy customers.

Here's another extremely vital point: what's the most important factor that makes a customer come in and buy from any business on a repeat basis? Is the lowest price the prime factor? Is it the one with the best quality? It is the business with the widest selection? Is it the business with the most persuasive advertising?

The answer is none of the above! The correct answer is this: scientific studies of customer buying behaviour show that the most important factor in a customer's decision to buy is HOW MUCH THEY LIKE AND TRUST THE SELLER!

This is a fact with tremendous implications. It means that if your customers like and trust you, they'll be willing to pay more just to do business with you. THAT MEANS YOU DON'T HAVE TO COMPETE ON THE BASIS OF PRICE! Yes, you can charge more than your competitors for the same product if you have established the reputation of a 'good guy' who cares deeply about customer needs.

Just think about the different outcome that could have been achieved in our first example about the computer store. Instead of trying to rifle £25 out my friend's pocket, the dealer should have been thinking: 'This chap has spent £10,000 here. I need him. I want to make sure he spends the next £10,000 here. To hell with my measly 25 quid! I've got to help this guy out now! When I solve his problem, he'll appreciate it!'

So don't be penny wise and pound foolish. Strive to create customers, and the sales will take care of themselves – oh yeah, and your sales will multiply magically as you build your list of repeat customers, along with your reputation as a people-oriented business that cares, not a profit hungry dealer who is willing to do anything to make a quid.

High octane 17

Didn't ask for it, didn't pay for it, but they got it anyway

There is only one thing a customer likes more than getting something for free – they like getting something for free they never expected to get!

What we're talking about here is added value. It's not advertised, it's not expected, it's not asked for, it's not paid for – but they get it anyway.

I know a car dealer that hands each new sold customer a coupon they can take to a nearby service station for a free tank of petrol. Is it so difficult to slide someone £30 or £40 worth of petrol after they just spent £20,000 on a new car? No, a tank of petrol isn't that much, but the customer remembers little things like that. They'll come back and spend their next £20,000 right there. It's amazing how £40 can get you £20,000 sometimes!

Publisher, author and big-time mail order success Russ Von Hoelscher advises: "...win success by giving your customers their money's worth. And if you really want great success, give your customers more than their money's worth."

Margaret Getchell of Macy's legendary department store in New York City says, "Be everywhere, do everything, and never fail to astonish your customers."

And super successful copywriter and author Bob Bly says, "(Giving something extra) doesn't mean you should give away your ideas and work for free. Far from it. But giving a little extra shows your clients that you genuinely care about their business success and want to help them."

Bob Bly also tells this story from his practice: "I was asked to write a brochure about a new software product – so new it had not been named yet. Although the client didn't ask for it, I submitted a list of names along with the manuscript. They didn't use any of the names. But they were appreciative, and my next assignment was even bigger ... not a bad investment for 20 minutes spent writing a few suggestions on a sheet of paper."

It doesn't have to be big, expensive or a drain on your bottom line. It just has to be a small gesture, a surprise added value that the customer notices, didn't expect, but appreciates greatly.

- If someone buys a £100 pair of athletic shoes from you, why not throw in a can of water-repellent spray to help protect the shoes?

- If you install a carpet for someone, why not give him or her a gift certificate for a free cleaning? Incidentally, you can cut a deal with the professional carpet cleaning service to provide low-cost or free cleanings in exchange for the business you shove their way!

- If a woman comes in and pays you £35 for a hair colouring and perm, why not give her a free bottle of shampoo available only in salons? She may just come back to buy a few dozen more bottles, and also give keep coming to you for all her future hair-styling needs.

Surprise your customers with added value they don't expect to get. You'll be amazed at how £5 will get you £500, or £5,000 time and time again!

High octane 18

Seven ways to turn shoppers into buyers

If you spend a ton of money on marketing techniques to get people to come into your place of business, wouldn't it be a shame if they just turned around and went out again without buying anything? It would be more than a shame, it could be a downright tragedy.

So here are seven ways to make sure that people who come in to shop also end up buying.

1. Ride the bronco.

Did you know that the average rodeo star is able to stay on a bucking bronco for only about eight seconds? Yet, most of the time, that's all they need to become champions. But shoppers can also buck off your business in eight seconds, and that means you win nothing. What do I mean? Studies show that shoppers take about eight seconds to decide whether they feel comfortable in your store, or not. This is based on a study of more than one million shoppers. This is why Sainsbury's supermarkets greet customers by asking them if they want a shopping cart or basket. The first thing the shopper confronts is a helpful, smiling person already caring about their needs. Wal-Mart stores in the USA have a 'greeter' at their doors.

2. Ensure the customer likes what he or she sees.

When a shopper comes in, if they don't like what they see right away – a dirty floor, bored, unhappy looking employees, disorganization – they are not likely to stay long enough to buy. Even a dirty car park can turn business away before they come in! Your store front is also key. It needs to look inviting. So what do people see when they come into your place of business? Make sure they feel comfortable and welcome and they're more likely to buy. Remember: you've got eight seconds!

You must look good, too. Not only should the outside and inside of your business look approachable, you and your employees must look approachable, too. Are you going to buy a car from a guy in a dirty (or even a clean) T-shirt? What if you walk into an insurance broker's office and you confront a receptionist with green hair, and an insurance broker wearing a loud, flowered shirt? If you're selling insurance to punk rockers, that might be okay, but how many punks are shopping for insurance these days?

3. Put a guarantee out front.

What if a prospect walks in and immediately sees your mission statement or guarantee prominently displayed? They might see: 'Our Mission: to do everything we can to satisfy our customers, or they pay nothing!' That's going to give them the instant confidence that they're going to get a fair shake in this place!

4. Know what prospects or shoppers want before they come in.

Send out a survey and ask people what they want. This strategy has double impact. If you send out a survey, that survey form can also be a sales letter. Thank them for filling out the survey by asking them to come in for something free, or a discount. Based on what your prospects tell you, you'll be ready to have what they asked for when they come in, and they will come in because you have motivated them to do so. And, oh yes, they'll also buy.

5. Capture all information possible.

When prospects or shoppers come in, capture all the information you can about them. Get name, address, phone number, and note what they bought. A computerized check-out system can do this for you. But if you get even more information, you can do even more. For example, if you find out the customer's birthday, you can send them a surprise congratulations card, along with a discount coupon as a 'birthday present.' When you honour and surprise people, and treat them like family, they come in and buy more often. Even if they don't buy the first time, getting their info can help you make them come back to buy.

6. Do the bounce back.

When a customer comes in and buys, give them an immediate incentive to come back in and buy again. Some businesses provide coupons for specials available the following week which are given to customers when they come in and buy today. Even if a shopper does not buy, give them the bounce-back anyway. A sale later is better than no sale at all.

7. The power of thank you.

Think of 'thank you' as a major marketing tool. How many times have you bought a car or an ice cream cone, and were given no thank you at all, or that automatic 'thanks' the check-out person mumbles without even thinking about it. That's not a real thank you. Neither are the words 'thank you' printed automatically in faded ink on the bottom of a check-out receipt. No, a real thank you is one the customer clearly hears and feels as a genuine gesture of appreciation. There are many good ways to do it. You can send out a hand-written card the same day of the purchase, thanking the customer with a personal note. You can call the customer in person, if you want to go all the way. Imagine the customer at home, answering the phone, and they hear you saying: "This is Mike Businessman of (business name). I just wanted to say thanks for coming in today, and wanted to make sure you're happy with your purchase." That's it. Don't attempt any more hard sell. A thank you is a gesture of appreciation, and not to be weighed down with more business plugs. When a customer gets this kind of personal attention, they'll become just that – a customer, and a repeat customer.

 High octane 19

The power of being 1st... and being 2nd!

Okay, quiz time. Who was the first man on the moon? That's easy: Neil Armstrong! Now, who was the second man on the moon? Do you know?

Who was the first man to sail the Atlantic to discover the New World? Easy Again! Christopher Columbus! Now, who was the second man? Hmmmm?

Who was the first pilot to break the sound barrier, or Mach I? That's Chuck Yeager. Who was the first man to break Mach II? Any idea?

What's my point? This: if you want to be remembered and well known, being first is an almost unbeatable publicity strategy. Everybody knows and remembers who did what first, but all those 'seconds' quickly fade into the footnotes of history.

WHO WAS THE SECOND MAN ON THE MOON? DO YOU KNOW?

Thus, if you want a market position that will be all but unassailable be the first! Now, you may be thinking this is a tall order. After all, not just anyone is going to become the next Coca-Cola, Range Rover or IBM! (Although you can try!) But the position of first can still work for you on a smaller scale.

For example, if you are the first to tell your customers something they did not know before, you'll get a competitive advantage. Or, be the first to do something different with your product, and you'll get a leg up on the competition.

A photographer can be the first in town to offer 'glamour shots.' An insurance intermediary can be the first to offer rebates on income protection insurance policies. If you tell everyone loudly enough, they'll see you as the innovator, the first to offer this or that. The second guy to offer it? He'll be forgotten.

Think about how you can be the first to offer something the others do not. And even if they do offer it, you can be the first to blow your horn about it – and you'll be perceived as a first. You'll gain a fantastically strong advantage over your competitors!

But wait a minute! What about being second? Can there be an advantage to this position, too? Indeed it can if you play your cards right. For example, the second man to make the trip to the New World after Columbus was Amerigo Vespucci. Here's what's interesting about that: the whole continent was eventually named after him – Amerigo – America! It wasn't named Columbia!

If being first is so important, how did Amerigo so successfully steal Columbus' thunder? Well, after his astonishing discovery of America, Columbus ended up an abject failure. He was a terrible businessman, and was unable to capitalize on his fame and amazing feat. Columbus died bankrupt and in prison. Amerigo, on the other hand, went on to publish a series of fantastically successful books about his adventures and journey to the New World. Within a very short time, Amerigo was the man associated with the discovery of the New World, while Columbus was forgotten, at least for a few decades. The bottom line was that Amerigo was a much better publicity man than Columbus.

Many companies today have actually used their position as second to make them stand out from the famous first, as did old Amerigo. For example, the car rental company Avis slogan was: 'Avis: we try harder!" They also made it known they were the second biggest next to Hertz in car rental. Their slogan was clearly aimed and suggested they 'tried harder' than the smug, complacent 'big guy' – Hertz!

Suddenly, Avis turned its inferior status into a marketing advantage. They made themselves look like a plucky underdog, taking on the complacent Big Guy. Everybody loves to pull for the underdog. It seems like they try harder, and are willing to do things the established No. 1 isn't in order to win over new business. If you're a second – or even in tenth – position yourself as 'the smaller guy who is trying harder.' People will love it.

2 HIGH OCTANE MARKETING

THINK ABOUT HOW YOU CAN BE THE FIRST TO OFFER SOMETHING THE OTHERS DO NOT

Answers!

The answer to the famous seconds are: Edwin 'Buzz' Aldrin was second on the moon. Amerigo Vespucci, of course, was second to the New World. The pilot who broke Mach II was Scott Crossfield. I knew you wanted to know! And, okay, I'll grant you that Leif Erikson clearly made it to the New World 500 years before Columbus did!

JUST LOOK AT ALL THE EXAMPLES OF STRATEGIC ALLIANCES AROUND YOU. MCDONALD'S RESTAURANTS SELL ONLY COCA COLA... AND IN TURN MAKES HUGE PROFITS ON IT BECAUSE THEY GET IT MUCH CHEAPER.

3 Joint marketing

Call it anything your want – strategic alliance, joint venture, fusion marketing, host-beneficiary deals, co-op marketing – as long as you do it!

Everybody in business makes a lot of noise about competition. You have to beat the competition, blow away the competition, out-think the competition, stay ahead of the competition. You need to 'get the competitive spirit.' You must 'position yourself against the competition.' In school we learn about 'survival of the fittest' and how species of animal compete. Only the strongest competitor wins! And we all know that free market capitalism is based on competition.

Even I beat the 'competition' drum a lot. But sometimes, we need to take a step back and take a whole new look at things if we are going to succeed, and find new ways to sell more and make more money. For the next few pages, I want to invite you to think not competition – but its opposite – cooperation!

In today's economy, it's more difficult than ever for anyone, especially the small business, to go it alone. It costs more to pay for all your own advertising, find all your own customers and do everything using only your own resources. There's an alternative: cooperating with and forming strategic alliances with other businesses. This enables you to pool resources, share customers, spread the cost of marketing, and do it in a way in which all parties win.

Wouldn't it be great if you could have instant access to a couple thousand of another company's customers? You can with a cooperative approach. That's why some people call this idea 'fusion marketing – because you and another business pool resources and work together for mutual benefit.

The idea of a joint venture or a strategic alliance is not to get married, but rather, to 'date' each other now and then help each other make bigger profits, while you both remain distinct business entities.

A strategic alliance with another entity can be simple and limited, to very involved and complex. Here are a few examples of a simple cooperative venture:

1. A car dealer approaches a local office supplies company and offers to pay for some of the cost of mailing its monthly invoices – if the office supplies company agrees to enclose an advertisement for the car dealer along with the bill. Both win. The car dealer gets a much cheaper way to distribute direct mail, and also gets access to a large number of potential customers. The office supplies company gets to lower its postage expense. (Also, the envelope is guaranteed to be opened because it's a bill! One of the biggest challenges of direct mail is getting the prospect to open it and read it!)

2. A dentist agrees to recommend or endorse an accountant to each of his dental customers. In exchange, the accountant pays a commission to the dentist for each new customer which results from the agreement. Again, both win. The accountant gets more customers, and the dentist makes money on the side merely for endorsing the accountant.

3. A copywriter approaches a web-based business that sells mail-order products, and asks the website owner to post his copywriting service somewhere on the website. Each client that comes to the copywriter via the website earns a commission for the website owner. Both win for obvious reasons. Also, the website owner has enhanced his product because he or she is offering more services on his or her page. If the copywriter specializes in writing copy for mail order products, the alliance is an even better match.

Strategic alliances can also be more complex and involved. Here's an example:

A group of 20 businesses form an organization that meets once a month so that all 20 can brainstorm strategic alliances with each other. A convenience store might make a deal to provide shelf space for a video rental store, a fitness centre can place 'take-one' boxes in which any one of the other businesses can place their fliers. This group of 20 can also sponsor its own community involvement program to help charities and other good causes. By pooling resources, significant money can be raised – and those who receive the money can be the core customers of all 20 members. Then each company can remind everyone, including the media, about all the good works they are doing. This will result in free press for all 20, and will touch individuals on a personal level. This can create powerful word-of-mouth advertising. That kind of reputation and image enhancement is all but priceless.

Be sure that whatever company you choose to make an alliance with is one that you would be proud to be associated with. If you make a deal with a shady dealer, some of that stink could easily rub off on you.

There are dozens of ways to cooperate with other businesses. You can trade mailing lists with others. A car dealer can recommend a mechanic, if the mechanic tells all of its customers that the car dealer has the best, most mechanically reliable cars in town. A hypnotherapist can tell his or her clients that getting a massage at ABC Health Centre will enhance relaxation and make the hypnosis process more potent because relaxation is key to being hypnotized properly and deeply!

Just look at all the examples of strategic alliances around you. McDonald's restaurants sell only Coke with their burgers. Coke not only gets an exclusive, mega-selling partner to move billions of gallons of product, but Coke also ends up in all of the McDonald's advertising. Coke pays nothing for this, yet reaps the benefits. McDonald's, in turn makes huge profits on Coke because they get it much cheaper than it would without the strategic alliance based on mutual benefit.

Here are the eight major facets on which companies can work together on:

1. Sharing costs of advertising and other marketing.

2. Logistics (airlines carry overload parcels for international couriers.)

3. Packaging (milk cartons carry the advertisements for other products and businesses.)

4. Product design (IBM computers use to recommend only Microsoft software.)

5. Selling (buy only X brand washing powder with this model of washing machine.)

6. Service (carpet fitter recommends carpet cleaner.)

7. Geographic proximity (business furniture retailer sends customers across the street to buy business office supplies, such as paper, pens, etc.)

8. Pricing (buy a dinner for four at the Italian restaurant and get a discount on a haircut at X.)

Start writing down the names of other companies which may be a perfect match for what you sell. Brainstorm for creative ways to help each other. Then pick up the phone, ask for a meeting, and map out your strategy. Thousands of customers may be only a phone call away from you at this minute! You won't need to buy advertising or telecanvasing, or anything else! Your future partner can give it all to you free – and you can give to them in return!

That's the beauty of cooperation!

A COUPON THAT A PROSPECT CAN CLIP AND SEND IN ALSO INCREASES RESPONSE...
IT WILL COST YOU SOMETHING, BUT MAKE YOU SO MUCH MORE.

4 Gold marketing principles

What if you could examine thousands of the best, response-pulling ads from the past century, and find out just why they worked so well?

What if you could discover key marketing techniques that have made sales letters pull fantastic responses, and feel totally confident they would work for you too? What if you could uncover basic, fundamental principles of selling and promotion that just can't miss if only you try them yourself? What if you knew exactly how to write headlines that grab attention and don't let go, and better yet, sell products fast and easy?

All of the above would be priceless, wouldn't it? Does such information exist? You bet it does! The fact is, academics and marketing research eggheads have been examining, analyzing, comparing, testing and recording everything that has worked, and everything that has failed in the past 100 years, and they have distilled it all down to black and white information that people just like you and me can pick up, use and achieve spectacular sales success as a result.

In this chapter, I'm going to give you a compact, concentrated dose of the very best of the best in marketing 'truths' that you can use to help you make your highest business goals a reality. These 17 Marketing Principles are pure marketing gold. Learn these nuggets, pick them up, and place each shining chunk in your personal marketing arsenal, and you'll be well on your way to getting big customer response, and making big money in the world of business and marketing.

Gold marketing principle 1

Long copy outsells short copy

It's a basic fact: The more words you use and the more of the story you tell, the more likely you are to sell a prospect successfully. A six-page sales letter almost always outsells a 4-pager. A full sheet of paper almost always outsells a postcard. A 30-minute infomercial will outsell a 30- to 60-second ad by an outstanding degree. An 12cm x 12cm ad will outsell a small classified ad every time.

Why is this? Because people need all the relevant information to make informed buying decisions. They need to have every possible question answered. They need to be sold repetitiously and thoroughly. When a person no longer has any unknowns to be afraid of, and when they understand all the ways they will benefit if they buy, they will buy. The more words, space and time you have to tell the full story, the better you can get the job done, and the more successful you'll be.

This does not mean that smaller, shorter, less detailed marketing vehicles do not have their place. For example, a classified ad is a fantastic tool when used in a two-step method. Rather than trying to make a sale with a classified ad, instead use it to intrigue and direct your prospect into asking for your longer sales tool – sales letters, tapes, videos, whatever. If you try to make a sale directly with a classified ad, you're asking that little ad to do a lot of heavy

PEOPLE NEED ALL THE RELEVANT INFORMATION TO MAKE INFORMED BUYING DECISIONS.

lifting it probably can't handle. It's kind of like expecting a small car to win the Grand Prix. It's the wrong tool for the job. Rather, it's better to use the small car to drive to the race track, where you then get into your massive, powerful vehicle to run and win the race! A postcard sent through the mail is a superb way to entice prospects into asking for your full-blown sales package, which will get the real selling done.

So remember, long copy outsells short copy! Don't pin all your hopes on smaller marketing tools that can't get the job done by them-selves! Do what you need to do to tell the whole story, answer all questions, cover everything thoroughly, and you'll get the results you have to have to make money and sell products!

 Gold marketing principle 2

The freephone call, the discount coupon

Give a prospect any tiny reason to not respond, and they won't. What if you take out an ad and list a phone number for people to call, but that phone call is not free? Are they going to call? Maybe, but not many of them. The first thing they'll think is: 'That's a long distance call. That costs.' But if you had a free phone number, they have no reason not to call because they have nothing to lose. The research simply proves this point. Free phone numbers boost response in a big way because they remove an obvious negative for responding.

A coupon that a prospect can clip and send in also increases response. A coupon is something solid for the prospect to focus upon, take action with, and use to get a great deal. What's going to get a better response – a sales letter with a discount coupon, or a sales letter without one? The answer seems ridiculously obvious, yet how many marketers fail to apply this simple technique? Just about all of them! But you're not going to make this mistake. A coupon will cost you something, but make you so much more.

A note of dissent: some high-powered marketing gurus actually frown on the freephone number in some cases. For example, Harvard educated marketing millionaire Dr. Jeffery Lant says a toll-free (free phone) number can be a bad idea for some people, such as consultants. Why? Because a freephone number tends to attract a lot of poorly qualified customers who are not serious about buying. Since the call costs nothing, many just dial it up and start blabbing with no real intent to buy. The result is that you waste a lot of time while making no money! On the other hand, if someone is interested enough to accept the cost of the phone call, they are probably highly motivated to be a serious customer.

The way you tell is this: if you are mass marketing large numbers of items, you probably want a freephone number to boost response. If you are a professional or consultant who works with people one-on-one, a freephone number may not be a good idea. A consultant sells his or her time and knowledge. Since you pay for the freephone service, a freephone call means you give away some of that time and knowledge on your own tab. The higher the ticket price and the fewer the customers, the less attractive a freephone number becomes… sometimes.

Gold marketing principle 3

A picture is not worth a thousand words

Should you include a photograph in your ads? Most of the time, the answer is no. Why? Well, what does a photo really do except show something? Merely letting a prospect see what something looks like is not selling. While it's true that a photo can be a piece of the puzzle in a total marketing message, the problem is that it takes up a lot of space – space you could be using to list benefits, make a great offer, explain to your customer why they should buy, and what they'll get if they do. So why do you see so many ads with photos in them? The vast majority of these ads are run by mega-corporations doing institutional advertising. The Ford Motor Company can afford to spend millions printing and publishing pictures of their shiny cars. They have a lot more money to also put in all the other marketing messages they want, even though they very often never do.

But you don't have that kind of money to blow. That means taking up a huge portion of your ad space with a big picture that just sits there and says nothing is a dangerous way to advertise.

In some cases, pictures can help, if they are used wisely, and they do not crowd out the more vital information that the ad copy delivers.

Here's another interesting point: when you send a sales letter, adding a picture of yourself somewhere may actually help response. That's because when you show your face, people are more willing to trust what you're saying in your letter. The reader thinks that if you're willing to show your face, you're most likely willing to stand behind your offer. Also, putting your picture on your business card is an excellent idea. It almost turns your tiny business card into a response-pulling piece of direct mail!

So think about your ad illustrations wisely, and that goes for your other printed marketing material as well.

Gold marketing principle 4

Avoid 'Glittering Generalities'

When you make superlative, grandiose, and general statements, they mean nothing and sell nothing. Here's some examples: 'The Best Deal In Town!'; 'A Great Product at a Fantastic Price!'; 'Super High Quality!'; 'We Buy in Bulk and Pass On Those Savings to You!'; 'Quality and Service.'

People have heard these kind of claims so many times, they are all but invisible. They put people to sleep. They trigger nothing in the brain. The cure for glittering generalities is to get specific. Give prospects an exact idea of what you're offering. 'You Lose 18 Pounds in 36 Days, or Your Money Back!' 'Fuel Additive Increases Mileage by 44%!' 'Car Insurance up to 16% Cheaper than Your Current Policy Guaranteed!' 'Studies Prove Product Lasts 136% Longer.'

Now you're giving something people can see, hear and think about. When you give people exact information, they are motivated to buy to get that specific benefit you're talking about.

WHEN YOU MAKE SUPERLATIVE, GRANDIOSE, AND GENERAL STATEMENTS, THEY MEAN NOTHING AND SELL NOTHING

Gold marketing principle 5

Positive outsells negative

It's a big mistake to market the fear factor, or any other negative factor. Every day, many marketers make the mistake of thinking that they can scare, threaten, or worry people into buying. The vast majority of the time, this approach fails. Making people feel good makes them buy. Making people feel bad turns them off. If an auto body repair company runs a big picture of a smashed up car, people are going to see a smashed up car and think of that company and associate the two. It's better to show a beautiful car that people would be proud to own. That's what you want your company to represent. Imagine a large picture of a face filled with acne in an ad for a skin cream. Does it turn people on? No, people want a fresh, healthy looking face, so show them one, and tell them that your product delivers this.

On the other hand: there are some correct ways to use negative images or messages, such as in 'before and after' pictures. A fat body on one side and a thin, muscular one on the other shows how to go from bad to good. That's okay.

Also, consider this: the mouthwash Listerine had tremendous success with an ad slogan that said: 'The Taste You Hate Twice a Day.' Why did this obviously negative statement about its own product work so well? Well, the Listerine people reasoned that there was no getting around the fact that their mouthwash tasted bad. So rather than trying to hide from it, they laid their cards on the table. The effect was one of a company being honest and straightforward. It also implied that, if a mouthwash is going to be powerful enough to kill germs, it must taste like harsh medicine. It also implied that all those other sweet tasting mouthwashes lacked the proper strength to get the job of cleansing a mouth done right.

Sometimes, when you make a negative statement about your own product, it gets people to open their minds and pay attention. 'You'll pay more, but you'll get more.' But make the negative statement about your own product, and do not direct it outward at the prospect.

Here's another example of a negative ad campaign that worked wonders. It was a US ad for Fram oil filters. A TV commercial featured a cranky car mechanic doing major, expensive repairs on a car. The tired, irritated looking mechanic tells viewers something like: "This car needs $1,500 in repairs, and it could all have been prevented if they had used Fram oil filters. They cost more, but they protect better." And Fram's famous slogan was, again coming from the cranky mechanic: "You can pay me now, or pay me later!" Then he shakes his head and gets back to work under the car. The ad ran for years and sold millions of high-priced oil filters.

So in general, avoid negative advertising. But if you do, use it in the right way, and be very careful! A negative ad can easily backfire!

Gold marketing principle 6

A sales letter must look like a letter

They're called sales LETTERS for a good reason. They're supposed to be a letter. They're not a brochure, an advertisement or anything else. The best marketing tools are those that don't look like marketing tools. The more your sales letter looks like a friendly, helpful missive from a friend, the more access you gain to the mind of the prospect. That means no fancy type styles, or super large fonts. Use 9, 10 or 11 point type. That's the size you see in your average newspaper. People are familiar and comfortable with it. Also, if you use type that is too large, you have to increase the size and bulk of your mailing which will cost you more.

Never use all capital letters. It's very difficult to read, it looks unnatural and people may even be offended by how 'loud' this makes your letter seem.

Yes, a sales letter has some aspects that an ordinary letter does not, such as a headline. Sales letters are also made better if certain, key phrases are underlined. It's even better to underline using a red pen. But these attributes work best when they are understated and subtle. A great sales letter is never complete without a P.S. and a super easy-to-use order form.

But as a general rule, make your sales letter look like a letter that has been typed up by a friend at a kitchen table. The results will speak for themselves.

Gold marketing principle 7

Sell solutions

It's been the magic key to riches for literally centuries, and it's still true today. If you can identify a common problem and offer a believable solution, you have a winning proposition on your hands. Marketing research is solid about the fact that people will eagerly buy something if it will solve their problem. Will it help me lose weight? Will it grow hair? Will it lower monthly bills? Will it make me safe? Will it make me popular? If you can convince your customers your product will do these kinds of things – just name your price.

Also remember this: in general, people don't buy to prevent problems they don't yet have. In general, prevention does not sell, but cure does – although this is not universally true. In an earlier example, I told you about a successful ad campaign for a car oil filter that was sold on the basis that it would prevent engine damage. It worked. There are certain things people want to avoid, so they'll buy if they think a product will cover them. Another good example of this is a product that makes septic tanks less likely to sustain damage. You just poor it down the drain and it works its magic, somehow, in your underground septic system. Another successful ad campaign in the U.S. featured an actor portraying a plumber conducting massive repairs in the back of someone's house. The entire yard was dug up to get at the buried septic tank. The plumber states that the procedure could run as high as $20,000, but a $5 box of the septic treatment stuff could have prevented it all. So this is another example of prevention selling well.

To sell prevention, you have to have a product that fits just right – it must protect something people have a very high degree of concern about, like a car, or a home. Otherwise, concentrate on selling the cure, and you'll sell well.

Gold marketing principle 8

The law of repetition

The vast majority of first-time sales people take one shot at a prospect and then give up to find another prospect to sell to until they are unsuccessful. When many beginners send out their first mailing of a sales letter and get poor results, they give up. Or they run an ad once and never try it again if it doesn't pull.

This is a tragedy! Experienced marketers know that first-time contacts are almost always the poorest in terms of positive response. The fact is, prospects need to be pitched two, three, four or even five times before they decide to buy. Never send a sales letter without having a second mailer ready to go a week or two later, and a third one after that, and even a fourth if response is still not adequate. You can't really judge how well an ad works if it runs only once. That's just not a proper test. It's a well-known fact that an ad may have to run three to six times in the same place before people really 'see' it.

I have a college instructor friend who was hired by a publishing company to write a college textbook. This is the formula they wanted him to use in writing the book:

1. Tell them what you are going to tell them.
2. Tell them.
3. Then tell them what you told them.

Why this formula? Because experienced educators know that students learn best when difficult concepts are hammered into their brains by repetition! Some studies show that a student must confront a concept up to eight times before they absorb it and really learn it!

Much the same is true in marketing. Why do you see the same commercials on TV running over and over again, until you're truly sick of seeing it? It's because marketers know that the more time the spot runs, the better it will be implanted into the brains of the consumer. It's better to risk irritating people with repetition than to give up too soon and make no sales.

Advertising also has a cumulative effect. Ads build up their audience, penetration and power the more times they run. Yes, if you're running a poorly constructed ad, you can run it a thousand times and get poor results. But you'll never really know how good or bad an ad is until you give it a chance by running it several times.

Does it cost more money to repeat? Absolutely not! It costs less to conduct repetitive marketing techniques because you make more money when your effort starts clicking. If you run an ad once and it bombs, you've lost that money for good, unless you try again! That's expensive! This doesn't mean you should try a different angle or a new approach – but you have to keep hitting away until you break through.

The law of repetition applies to all forms of selling – from face-to-face sales, to telephone sales, to direct response marketing through the mail.

All this reminds me of a great aphorism: 'Call a man a dog once, and you insult him. Call a man a dog a thousand times and he may start barking!'

PROSPECTS NEED TO BE PITCHED TWO, THREE, FOUR OR EVEN FIVE TIMES BEFORE THEY DECIDE TO BUY

Gold marketing principle 9

Customers come first

Too many entrepreneurs focus on making sales, sales, sales. But what they should be focused on is making customers, customers, customers! Because when you concentrate on customers, the sales take care of themselves.

What exactly am I talking about here? It's not rocket science – it's the common sense idea that if you strive to make people happy, they'll buy from you, and better yet, they'll keep buying from you.

A lot of less-than-scrupulous marketers are playing the game of 'Gotcha!' What they do is put together a marketing message that is loaded with hype, which promises the moon, and then they deliver an inferior product. The vast majority of customers blame themselves for believing an ad that sounded too good to be true. They lick their wounds, say good-bye to their money – and they never buy from you again. Some sellers even make a lot of money this way, but eventually, their business runs out of fuel. That's because they constantly need to find new prospects whom they have not ripped off before. That's expensive. Each new customer means having to buy more ads, send out more mailers, and all the rest. Even that gets more difficult because all those unsatisfied customers out there are spreading a negative word-of-mouth advertising campaign against you.

Even in a market with millions upon millions of people, it's amazing how fast a single seller can gain a widespread reputation as being less than nice to deal with.

But when you do the opposite – when you bend over backwards to guarantee customer satisfaction – the payback is absolutely enormous. A happy customer will go out of their way to buy from you again. Happy customers ignite a positive word-of-mouth campaign about your business, which piles on even more sales. That positive word-of-mouth advertising costs you nothing, but gains you everything.

Sometimes you lose money in your attempts to make a customer happy. For example, you may have to give a full refund. You may even have to send a customer to a competitor if you can't sell that person what they need to solve their problem right now. But never be short-sighted about this. When you make a customer happy in this way, the payback is incredible. This is a solid marketing fact! If you lose money on a customer the first time by solving a problem, it's an iron-clad guarantee that this customer is going to come back to you and buy again – they will even be willing to pay a lot more just to do business with you. And don't forget the lifetime value of each customer. That's the amount of money they will spend with you over a period of months or years. A customer is more than just one sale – they are a potential string of sales that keep coming month after month. When you take time to calculate how much a customer is worth to you based on repeat sales and future business, it makes perfect sense to keep that customer happy in the long term, and not be overly concerned about only that first sale.

Gold marketing principle 10

It's perception, not product

It's one of the oldest marketing principles: 'Build a better mouse trap, and people will beat a path to your door.' The only trouble with this famed principle is that it is not true. In the end, it's not the best product that wins the marketing game. It's the product with the perception of being the best that wins. That's a subtle but important distinction!

Remember this: the perception in the mind of the consumer is reality. Your product is not reality. Your product is only as good as people perceive it to be, no matter how good or bad it is.

For example, let's look at two popular competing brands of soup. In the United Kingdom, Heinz is the undisputed dominant brand. But in the United States, Heinz soup sells very poorly, and is even unknown to most Americans. Campbell's soup is the undisputed No. 1 soup in America, yet has never been able to compete with Heinz in Britain.

Both companies have conducted rigorous scientific testing of their soups in both countries. In totally blind, objective taste tests, neither the British nor the Americans could tell the difference between either brand of soup. In other words, science has proved that both Heinz and Campbell's are exact equals of each other in taste, for all intents and purposes.

Yet, why do Americans refuse to buy Heinz and why do Brits snub Campbell's? The only answer is that this phenomenon is an artefact of the mind – it's all about perception. Americans PERCEIVE Campbell's to be better, even though in blind taste tests they couldn't tell the difference. The same is true in the UK. The citizens of both countries have made up their minds, and once they do, changing it is extremely difficult.

So what does this tell us? It shows how vitally important the perception of your product is. It means that the 'reality' of the mind is far more important that the 'reality' of the physical product itself. Thus, your marketing effort is a battle of perceptions. You must strive to win the minds of consumers more than you do anything else.

Many marketers take cynical advantage of this. They produce a second rate product, and then pour tons of advertising and marketing effort into convincing people that the product is good. If they succeed, they win. That may not be fair, but that's the way it is.

Does this mean you don't have to worry about quality? Well, yes and no. Your product must be at least equivalent to your competitors. A truly shoddy product will eventually expose itself to be what it is – junk. But the bigger lesson here is the overwhelming importance of building the perception that your product is the best. You do that with your marketing messages, with repetition, with promotion and all the rest. When you're thinking about how to best present your product, always think 'mind' first and 'objective reality' second. This means concentrating on 'benefits' and not features. Benefits are what the product will do for the customer. A feature is an attribute of the product itself. People don't care what your product is made from, they only want to know what it will get them: love, prestige, happiness, satisfaction, relief – not one of these is a solid 'thing' – yet that's what people want to buy.

Keep the rule of perception in mind, and you'll cut closer to where the real battle for the customer is fought and won – in the mind.

Gold marketing principle 11

Free advertising is a must

What would it be like to try win a ten mile foot race while you were wearing high-heeled shoes, and everyone else athletic shoes? Think you have a chance of winning? Not likely!

The same is true of the business that wants to rely on paid advertising alone. With paid advertising, you can only get so far so fast. You may do well enough to make a profit, but it's tough. To make your business really take off, you must implement free advertising strategies – you must use promotional techniques that generate widespread positive awareness of your business and product. That means getting articles written about your product in newspapers, and stories about your product on TV and radio. It also means getting strong word-of-mouth advertising going about your business.

Most experienced business people report that as much as 90% of their new business comes not from paid advertising, but from referrals. And what is a referral but a free word-of-mouth plug? Now imagine taking away that 90% of new business, and think about what it does for the bottom line of the business. When you think about it that way, all this seems obvious, right?

So get your publicity machine in gear and drive it hard! You must send out press releases, you must put on public events for the press to attend, you must do something newsworthy to get attention. And perhaps most important of all, you must ignite a word-of-mouth campaign. You do that by 'bribing' and asking all your customers to refer you to another customer, and another, and another. You also do that by providing extraordinary customer service. You want to please people so much that they'll tell others about it. Keep doing it enough, and you just won't believe how many new customers come seemingly out of nowhere to buy from you.

Remember, advertising you have to pay for is expensive, and very often, that expensive advertising does not work! But free advertising works like magic just about every time, and all the business you get from it is profit you've gained without needing to pay someone else to get it.

 Gold marketing principle 12

Use salt to make them thirsty

Here's another old saying: 'You can lead a horse to water, but you can't make him drink.' Is it true? Well, it's only true if you don't know anything about motivation. The fact is, you can make a horse drink every time if you know how to motivate it – how about putting some salt in the horse's oats! That'll get old Nelly drinking!

The same problem confronts businesses everyday. A good ad may bring droves of people into the store – only to see them look around and leave without buying anything. The problem is, you have led your horses to the water, but you could not motivate them to drink! So how do you do it?

You do it by getting their interest, then adding salt to intensify that interest, and then make the only way to satisfy the interest is to take action and buy.

For example, let's say you're selling a book on how to get easy credit. Here is a lukewarm way to conjure up reader interest in a sales letter:

'In *The Book of Easy Credit*, you will learn:

- How to get an unsecured credit card.
- How to go after venture capital.
- How to convince a banker to give you a loan.
- How to get a government grant.

And so on ...'

Now here is the 'salty' way to sell this same product:

'*The Book of Easy Credit* reveals more than 104 amazingly easy and little known ways to get credit from sources we guarantee you have never heard about!

You will learn:

- Where millions in untapped money is waiting for you right now in this one underused resource, page 83.
- The three things you must know to get a credit card, even with a bad credit rating, page 47.
- Six 'magic' statements that will get a banker to accept your loan application every time, page 104.
- The seven deadly kinds of credit you absolutely must avoid, page 137.
- Which government agency is most likely to give you a grant, and why, page 98.

And so on...'

In the first example, the sales copy simply tells the prospect what they will get, which is not all that bad – it's just not as salty as it could be! In the second example, the copy teases the reader. It hints at the tremendous knowledge they'll get if they buy, but they have to buy to find out. Better yet, it makes the reader curious. Just what are those six magic statements you can tell a banker? Which credit sources must I avoid?

Salting your marketing messages is very much akin to 'selling the sizzle and not the steak.' If you make the prospect salivate at the smell and the sound of the steak on the grill, they'll be motivated to buy and get the steak itself. So how can you salt your marketing communication? Just remember, without a little salt, the horse will only drink when it wants to!

 Gold marketing principle 13

Hit close to home

Here is a gold principle for people who are selling face-to-face or door-to-door. When you zero in on an individual, and hit that person where they can really feel it, you have made a connection, and a sale will almost always follow. What do I mean by this?

Here's an excellent example: one of the best salesmen I ever knew got his start in the brutally difficult job of selling vacuum cleaners door-to-door. Ask anyone who has tried selling vacuum cleaners and you'll hear stories of woe and rejection like no other. Yet, my friend found selling vacuum cleaners incredibly easy – even though he was selling an expensive model with a price tag of almost £1,000! How did he do it?

"A SUCKER'S BORN EVERY MINUTE."
P.T. BARNUM OF BARNUM & BAILEY CIRCUS

He hit close to home. Here's what he did. Instead of doing what all vacuum cleaners sellers did – demonstrate how well the machine cleaned the living room rug – my friend convinced his prospects to let him vacuum their beds!

As it turns out, even a mattress that looks clean very often has an incredible amount of disgusting dirt and debris hidden on its surface. My friend spent a few minutes going over a mattress, and then shook out the bag on a piece of very white cloth, and then on a piece of very dark cloth. The result was a frightening amount of crud that no one ever imagined they were sleeping on every night. Both the white and black surfaces revealed different kinds of unhealthy looking junk that sent prospects into swoons of distress – after which they eagerly bought a cleaning machine!

What my friend was doing was hitting his prospects close to home – he showed them clearly how his product could affect a very personal part of their lives they may never have thought about before.

When you show your prospects in a very personal way just why they need what you have, they are going to buy. But you have to figure out where to hit them and it has to hit close to home.

Gold marketing principle 14

Never underestimate the intelligence of the buyer

Perhaps the greatest promoter of all time was P.T. Barnum of Barnum & Bailey Circus. Barnum is famous for having said: "There's a sucker born every minute." This is the philosophy he used to drive his show to astounding heights of prosperity.

The American columnist H.L. Mencken is considered one of the greatest writers and social observers of the previous century. He is famous for having said: "No one ever went broke by underestimating the intelligence of the American public."

The great British writer W. Somerset Maugham said: "When you consider how stupid the average person is, it should be no great compliment for anyone to be considered above average."

If we are to take the advice of these major figures of history, it would seem wise to treat our target markets like they were idiots, and feel free to do everything we can to trick them into buying whatever we want to sell them.

Is this true? In fact, this is NOT TRUE! Barnum, Mencken and Maugham have a right to their opinions, but they were men from another era. Especially today, the average customer is more sophisticated than ever. Listen to what Prof. Fairfax Cone of the Foote, Cone and Belding ad agency says:

"That woman in the supermarket isn't an idiot, she's your wife! And she's the smartest shopper in the world. There are 30,000 items on the supermarket shelves, and when one of them goes up a nickel, she knows it. So when you're writing your ads, don't treat her like an idiot, treat her with the respect she deserves!"

This means that you need to be straightforward in all your marketing efforts. If you expect to 'pull a fast one' on your buying public, sooner or later, it's going to catch up with you, and probably sooner.

If this is so, why then do we all see so many deceptive ads all the time, and why do we see them everywhere? The answer is obvious: the vast majority of those ads fail! Just because you see a lot of deceptive advertising does not mean that all those ads are successful. They simply are not. Yet, people never learn. Everyday, a new seller thinks he or she is going to make a killing with a less-than-honest ad campaign. Every day, those people crash and burn. They learn the hard way: deception and dishonesty do not pay!

If you want to succeed, never go down the road of deception, no matter how clever you think you're being. The public is a lot smarter than you think. So when you write your ads or direct marketing materials, don't make the mistake of thinking Barnum was right when he said "a sucker's born every minute." Rather, when you write your marketing materials, think of your wife, your brother, your husband, your parents, your best friends. These are the people you're trying to reach and trying to sell. How easy is it to fool these people who are close to you? Would you want to? I don't think so, and even if you did, you'd be making a mistake – and I think you know that.

Gold marketing principle 15

Why not bribe them?

There's nothing like a good old bribe to get what you want. How do big corporate Chief Executives get what they want from the government? They bribe them with money. They may call it a 'party contribution,' and it's all perfectly legal, but it amounts to the same thing.

How do you get your children to mow the lawn? You bribe them. You offer a crisp £5 note, or tickets to the cinema. Suddenly, the bored teenager is out there getting your lawn in shape!

Giving people something they want badly enough is a great way to motivate them to do what you want.

So why not bribe your customers? No, we're not talking about anything illegal. We're talking about motivating customers to get off their backsides, get out their wallets and buy from you!

There are a lot of good ways to bribe customers. Better yet, bribes work across the demographic chart – from small-time spenders to millionaires – everyone will go for a good bribe anytime. It's fundamental human psychology.

Marketing studies show that businesses of all kinds issue billions in bribes every year. They give away free caps, pens, paper weights, calendars, T-shirts, knick-knacks, free food, one free when you buy two – and it goes on and on.

Better yet, marketing studies show that 40% of people who get something free from a business remember the name of the advertiser – for up to one year later! That kind of name recognition is worth a little bribe now and then, don't you think?

HOW DO YOU GET YOUR CHILDREN TO MOW THE LAWN? YOU BRIBE THEM.

What about direct mail? Can you offer a bribe in exchange for an increased response? In fact, offers of inexpensive free stuff or discounts have been shown to increase direct mail response by a whopping 342%! When you boost direct mail by that amount, the pay-off is almost unbelievable!

Bribing can be applied to any kind of marketing tool you can think of. If you have a booth set up at a trade show, you'll get droves of people to visit if you display a large, easy-to-see bribe where everyone can see it. Maybe it's only a free cup of tea or coffee, a pen, or a 10% off discount coupon. The bigger the bribe, the better. People will take a minute to stop and get their little freebie. When you make sales calls by phone, if you offer a free £2 plastic watch (easily bought in bulk from wholesalers) to any who agree to take a chance on your product, positive results will skyrocket over a sales call that offers nothing but the product itself.

When considering your own bribes, ask these six questions:

1. How much money can I spend on bribes? Think of it as part of your advertising budget.

2. What kind of bribe will be most useful to my target market? Women like different things than men. Wealthy people have different tastes than less wealthy people. Young people have different interests from senior citizens. In other words, target market your bribes!

3. Is my bribe desirable? I've said it before, but I'll say it again – an offer for something free is just not good enough. That freebie must have value! You can't bribe people with something they don't want or can't use.

4. Can I come up with a unique bribe? What will make people stop and look twice, or think twice? If you have something people can brag about, they will often tell their friends: "Would you believe I got this free from so-and-so?" Now you have not only bribed an individual, you have prompted them to go out and give you word of mouth advertising.

5. How many people do I want to reach? You need to know because you need to determine how many bribe items you will need to give away.

6. What advertising message will accompany my bribe? Don't make a free offer, only to fail with the follow-through. You're going to spend some money on your bribes – be prepared to go for the kill to get maximum pay-back from them.

Where do you find good bribe items? There are many companies that specialize in creating 'give me' items, like pens, calendars, T-shirts, magnets, and more. All of these items can carry your phone number and advertising message. Look in the *Yellow Pages* under 'promotional items' or 'advertising specialties.' You'll find more than a few companies who will be more than glad to send you a catalogue of everything they offer. If you're going to make bribes, make them carry some extra weight by serving as a convenient place where your prospects can easily find your phone number. You can also develop your own bribes. Information products are great.

Reports, audio tapes, video tapes – these can be loaded with your marketing messages. A free video tape is a fantastic bribe. So is a CD with your DVD movie burned onto it. Just about everybody likes to look at a video, or pop a CD into their computer.

Bribes cost some money but they make much more!

Use bribes to:

1.   Motivate a prospect to ask for your marketing materials.

2.   Get prospects to fill out a survey.

3.   Get your sales staff selling like mad!

4.   Lure people to your booth at a trade show.

5.   Motivate people to buy more, larger, or more expensive.

6.   Advertise.

7.   Reward customers for buying, to say thank you, and to bolster repeat sales.

8.   Convince people to buy now!

9.   Lure people to your public lecture

10. Get free publicity. Get the press to play Santa Claus by letting them tell people where they can get something free.

11. Position yourself against the competition.

12. Make the competition look bad!

13. Build your image as an honest, generous dealer.

14. Increase phone sales.

15. Make all your print, radio and TV advertising many times stronger.

16. Get people to come to your web page, and make them buy while there.

17. Get rid of stockpile items you couldn't sell in the first place!

18.   Implant yourself into the minds of consumers – and make it stick for a year, or longer!

19.   Make an unhappy, unsatisfied customer come back to you.

20.   Get cheaper ad rates from media outlets.

21.   Make classified ads work like magic.

Finally, always test the results of your bribes! Because this strategy costs a bit of money, testing is more important than ever. You need your bribing strategy to work, and work powerfully. You can make it happen by carefully tracking results, and showing direct causation between bribe, sale and profit.

Gold marketing principle 16

The very best investment: yourself!

A friend of mine in the U.S. recently inherited about $20,000. He took $10,000 of it and bought stocks. He plunged $6,000 of the sum into a single company his stockbroker was so excited about, he told my friend he was putting his own money into it! The company was the telecommunications giant WorldCom. It was about to merge with another telecommunications giant, MCI. It was partially this impending merger that made WorldCom the darling of Wall Street.

My friend bought $6,000 at $42 a share.

A few months later, the US government regulatory agencies stopped the merger, saying it would create an illegal monopoly. WorldCom stock plunged. Since the very day he bought at $42, it went nowhere but down, yet, he decided to hang on. In the summer of 2002, WorldCom was caught in an accounting fraud scandal, and was forced to declare bankruptcy.

Just before WorldCom was delisted from the market, it was worth 9 cents. My friend's $6,000 was vaporized!

Why do I tell this depressing tale? To make a point. There are a lot of ways to invest your money, some relatively safe, some risky, as my friend found out. The high risk investments pay off big – maybe as high as 20 or 30% – if nothing scary happens, as it often does. Low risk investment is stable, but you're lucky if you get a low, double digit return. And let's not even talk about those dreadful interest rates the banks are giving hard-working people who have traditional savings accounts with them.

No, I say the best possible investment is yourself! What do I mean? Well, if you take your money and start a business, you suddenly have the opportunity and ability to make your money grow, not just percentage points, but exponentially. Here's an example:

I have another friend who has a freelance copywriting business. One day, he decided to write a short manual entitled, *How to Write Fast*. It took him a couple of long afternoons to write this short manual of about 35 pages.

Next he bought a small one-inch space ad for the manual in a popular writer's magazine with a national audience. The ad cost around £280. He offered the manual for £12, plus shipping. His cost to print and mail the manual was about £3 each, so he could expect a profit of about £9 per sale.

Two weeks after the magazine hit the news stands and was sent to all subscribers, my friend had received 236 orders. At £9 profit each, he netted more than £2,000 – £2,124.00 to be exact! After three months, the orders finally started to trickle down to just a few per week – but not until he had sold 1,139 copies for a profit of £10,251!

So just one £280 ad brought him £10,251 in just 90 days! If you're good at maths, go ahead and calculate what kind of percentage

INVEST IN YOURSELF. START A BUSINESS, CREATE A PRODUCT, BUY AN AD.

of return he received on his investment of £280 – but you don't need to do that to understand what I'm getting at here!

This single example shows the tremendous potential that can come from a good idea, a single ad, and a good idea.

You and your own marketing efforts are the best investment you can make! Furthermore, you are always in control. When you buy stocks, or any other investments, you have to sit back and hope that the markets, the corporate executives and others do well for you. Not so when you implement your own marketing plan. You take charge of your own life, and your own money.

Yes, your own marketing efforts can fail too. All marketing contains an element of risk. But when you fail, you also gain something. What? Knowledge! There really is no such thing as failure – only lessons to be learned. We all have to fail a number of times to achieve success. If you think of your own failures as mere 'course corrections' then you're going to keep swinging away until you hit a home run.

An ad that doesn't work is an excellent 'test.' You try another ad, try altering the headline, making a better offer, adjusting the price, and keep going until it clicks. When it does, you can easily get 1,000% back on your investment, and you don't have to wait six months for that interest to accrue! You get fast cash now! Then you take a portion of the money you earned and plunge it back into more marketing efforts: direct mail, radio ads, a mass distribution of flyers. More profits flow in!

So invest in yourself. Start a business, create a product, buy an ad. When you challenge yourself, when you put yourself at risk, you light a fire beneath your seat that'll get you going like nothing else. You'll also have a hell of a lot of fun along the way!

Gold marketing principle 17

Combining marketing tools multiplies their power

I know of a chap, whose primary mode of selling was the telephone because that's what he was comfortable with. He was selling a series of books and audio tapes that would help people accelerate the learning process with such tools as speed reading, memorization techniques and more. It was a terrific product and a system he developed himself while working as a college professor at a small university. He quit his job to focus on selling his accelerated learning program, hoping to turn it into a thriving business.

He was doing fairly well making sales by phone, earning just enough money to make it worth his while and pay his bills. But then it was suggested he could sell a lot more if he bought some radio advertising to pitch his product. The product seemed a good match for radio advertising. He agreed to try. He bought a series of radio ads that gave a strong pitch and announced a freephone number prospects could call. The ad ran periodically for almost two weeks in his city.

The problem was that his freephone number barely rang at all. The radio ads were a big flop. He was mortified and it cost him a lot of money, and got him little in return.

And yet all was not lost… His telephone sales suddenly quadrupled! As it turned out, hundreds of people had heard the radio ads, but few of them bothered to write down and call the number. But when he made his 'cold' sales calls, he was delighted to discover that a high number of his calls weren't so cold anymore! That's because a lot of them had heard the radio ads, had some time to think it over, and were ready to buy when he called. By adding radio advertising to his telephone sales strategy, he had managed to greatly increase the effectiveness of the latter.

The moral of the story: when you combine marketing techniques, they often increase the power of each other. In his case, the radio ads had worked to change the attitude of the public, softened them up, and got them ready to buy when he called.

The same is true of direct mail. When you follow-up a mailing with a phone call, response rates have been shown to increase from 6% to 22% or more! The results tend to be even stronger when direct mail is teamed up with print advertising.

If you are targeting a specific city, area or region, try buying a series of ads for your product and let them run for a couple of weeks. Then hit the same area with direct mailing, and you'll be amazed at the results.

Make sure your two or three different marketing tools have a definite connection with each other. Push the same benefit in a print ad as you do in the direct mail piece. If you call a prospect after mailing them, refer to what you told them in the mail piece, and increase the attractiveness of the offer even more.

WHEN YOU FOLLOW-UP A MAILING WITH A PHONE CALL, RESPONSE RATES HAVE BEEN SHOWN TO INCREASE FROM 6% TO 22%

Another good idea is to advertise a higher price in the first round of marketing, then follow-up with a lower price. Someone else I know of was selling a booklet on how to get government grants. In a four-page sales letter, he asked for $19.95. After about ten days, he sent a postcard to all those who didn't go for the $19.95 price, and offered the booklet for just $12.95. The response to the second, lower price was phenomenal! Interestingly, the lower price is the price that he wanted in the first place! He never expected to get $19.95, yet he still got a few from his initial mailing. But then a very high percentage bought at the lower price resulted in a very nice profit.

The effect was to make people think they were getting a $19 product for only $12. It's all just a matter of perception – but as you already know, in marketing, perception is everything.

I urge you to combine and coordinate your various marketing tools to multiply their power. This terrific technique easily completes my list of Marketing Gold Principles!

INVESTORS HUNGRILY BOUGHT UP SHARES OF ANY COMPANY WITH DOT.COM BEHIND ITS NAME...

AND SUDDENLY, THE BUBBLE BURST

5 Winning with e-commerce

Here's the thing about the Internet: the Genie is out of the bottle.

Yes, the E-Commerce Genie burst out of its bottle like a miraculous apparition over a decade ago.

It seemed to instantly takeover the world. It took everything we know about business and marketing and made it 'old news.' The old paradigm was swept out, and the new paradigm rushed in. Suddenly, no company without 'dot.com' behind its name could get an ounce of attention from the media. Venture capital and investment sources diverted their mighty flow away from passé 'brick-and-mortar' operations to the mighty new dot.com gods. Millions of millionaires were made overnight, many of them young computer geeks with no college educations, a large percentage of them not old enough to legally buy a beer. In a period of just five years, one million new millionaires were created by Internet based start-ups. Names like Amazon, Lastminute and Yahoo dominated our attention. Thousands of copycats scrambled to become the 'next Amazon.com' or the 'future Yahoo.' Investors bought dot.com shares faster than a pack of wolves chasing down a deer. The stock market swelled with new Internet-based companies, and stock market investors hungrily bought up shares of any company with dot.com behind its name.

And suddenly, the bubble burst. Just as Dorothy in *The Wizard of Oz* finally gets to meet the wizard, only to find a silly old man running a phoney smoke and mirrors show, the dot.com Genie turned out to be little more than a wisp of smoke curling from the top of a bottle. The Genie looked exciting and powerful, but he had no true power, no staying power, and he certainly wasn't able to just sweep away all that had come before him, replacing everything with a new way of doing business.

Thousands of dot.coms went bankrupt, taking down billions of investment money with them, and knocking stock markets back on their heels.

And what did those markets fall back on after the dot.com debacle? That's right! The markets were anchored by all those supposedly passé bricks-and-mortar operations that had fallen so disgracefully out of favour just a few years ago! You see, these old established companies had tangible assets –buildings, commodities, factories, fleets of transportation vehicles, ships, oil in the ground, infrastructure, solid bases of loyal customers, cash flow – all things most dot.com company owners were laughing at in their sadly brief heyday.

What did the dot.coms have? They had ideas. They had a new selling proposition and method. They had a new medium. They had the aura of a new exciting technology. They had a lot of theories.

Most of the dot.coms also had this extremely bizarre idea: profits are optional. Profits are not to be worried about. The downright cynical (if not criminal) strategy of most of the dot.coms was this: 'Let's get enough investors excited about what we say we can do, with the ultimate goal of issuing an IPO. After we become a publicly traded company, we'll all be millionaires. After that we don't care what happens!'

And we all know what happened.

In the end, an idea is not an oil well. An idea is not a cargo ship loaded with wheat. An idea is not a factory churning out cars, furniture, refrigerators, beef, lumber, televisions and steel. You can eat wheat, you can't eat an idea. Refined oil will keep your house warm in the winter, but an idea can't. You can build a skyscraper with steel – but with an idea?

Yes, a single idea can change the world – and has – but that idea has to be made into something real and tangible before it can change anything! And that's the lesson behind the spectacular rise and fall of the dot.com empires. They captured the world's imagination with new possibilities, new ideas, new ways of thinking. But, for the most part, they failed to go all the way. In the end, they didn't really produce anything. They only promised to make profits – and many didn't even do that!

Yet, and yes – the Genie is still out of the bottle! Nothing is going to stuff him back in! Furthermore, the Genie is not as powerless as all those bruised investors probably think he is. The fact is, the Internet HAS given us a new way of doing business, a new way of looking at things, and all kinds of exciting new possibilities. And to be fair, a few of those dot.coms have managed to come out the other end of the experiment as success stories. After almost nine years, Amazon.com finally reported its first quarterly profit. eBay is doing brisk business, and making a profit. Google has emerged as the massive search engine winner of choice on the Internet. It's a cash-rich operation. It makes a profit, and it's growing.

So the key to using the Internet and successful E-commerce is to embrace this exciting new technology, and ground it in the good old fashioned principles of marketing, such as:

- **Creating a high quality product or service.**
- **Selling something real.**
- **Serving customers.**

- Solving customer problems.
- Creating high traffic flow into the base of operation.
- Generating repeat business.
- Making great offers.
- Talking about benefits.
- Delivering fast friendly service.
- Having profit as a primary goal.
- Bamboozling the competition!

Despite the dot.com collapse, I strongly urge you to include Internet marketing in your overall business strategy – and indeed – you risk slipping behind others if you don't look to the Internet to see what it can do for you and your operation.

For starters, here's what a web-based platform can do for you:

- Introduce your business to thousands, or millions of new customers.
- Enable you to have a global presence – right from home!
- Sell your products.
- Create customer awareness.
- Learn customer needs and wants.
- Generate free publicity.
- Capture mailing lists and key customer information factors.
- Shape your image.

- Serve as a media release and publicity centre.

- Generate side income or additional income beyond your primary product.

- Handle market research, helping you uncover hidden sources of business.

And much more...

Let's discuss some of the important details of using E-commerce for gaining profit and solid marketing advantage.

Your website

There are right ways and wrong ways to create a website. Building an attractive website that people will want to visit again and again is already a refined art. That means you probably should hire professionals to design your site – but be careful! Many 'Web Heads' are very good at creating wiz-bang sites that are exciting, attractive and nice to look at – but that's not your primary goal. Your primary goal is to sell things and make a profit. Just as in advertising, you should never substitute the show for the sell. If lots of people have fun on your site, but never buy anything, you have failed in your mission to sell and make profits. Thus, you need to inform your professional web page designer that your burning goal is to make a site that is conducive to getting people to come, and getting them to buy. All else is secondary.

When your website is created, the first thing a customer should see is your unique selling proposition – that is, tell them how you will solve their problems, meet their needs, and give them the best deal they'll find anywhere, on or off the web. The customer must get an immediate idea that you have something for them that is going to benefit their lives in a real and solid way. Shoppers must get the idea that the only way to obtain those benefits is to buy as quickly as possible.

On the web, you have only seconds to get this job done. Internet surfers have attention spans even shorter that TV watchers! Clicking that mouse is just too easy. The shopper's finger is always on the clicker. There's always so many other endless, glittering choices to look at on the web, so you have to make your proposition and your offer with lightening speed.

To do this, we can take a lesson from writing good headlines. A headline at the top of the ad must grab attention quickly. It must make a promise. It must offer a solution to a problem, or hint at something that can be gained. If the headline fails, the rest of the ad is lost. If you don't get attention with the headline, the reader is not going to go further into the ad to read your body copy, where the real sale is made. The same is true of your opening webpage. It must hook and grab the surfer without delay. Then you lure them deeper into the site content, where you make your best sales pitch.

Netting the market

People must be able to find your site. Today, that still means aggressive search engine placement. The higher your webpage gets placed on search engine results, the more hits you get. High search engine placement is something of a science in itself, and going into it in great detail goes beyond the scope of this book. But there's plenty of good information out there on how to do it. Also, your web designer and other consultants can help you get strong search engine results. You can also pay many search engines to guarantee

A HEADLINE AT THE TOP OF THE AD MUST GRAB ATTENTION QUICKLY. IT MUST MAKE A PROMISE.

your high placement – a controversial practice, yet perfectly legal, if not an inexpensive strategy. Google 'AdWords' is an example of this that you may want to consider.

You must also aggressively promote your site off-line. Put your web address on all your marketing communications: your ads, business cards, letterhead, brochures. Use classic networking techniques to spread the word about your site – tell everyone you meet that you have a new website and ask them to go take a look, and also ask them for their opinion. When you send out a sold product, include a bonus or coupon if they will go to your site and have a look. Take out dirt-cheap classified ads to promote your site. This is the classic 'two-step' method used by direct marketers. The classified prompts a reader to request more in-depth marketing materials – and nothing is deeper than a well designed webpage loaded with all the copy, facts, information and answers people need to make informed buying decisions.

You should also seek affiliate arrangements with other websites, which I'll discuss more in a while.

Getting them to stay and come back

Once you get a strong traffic flow coming to your website, the real work begins! It's not enough to get them to come – you must get them to stay, to buy, to come back again, and even get them to recommend your site to others, generating that all-important word-of-mouth advertising.

We've already touched on how you get people to stay and buy. You hook them quickly with a high-profile promise of benefits, similar to the way a headline grabs a reader of a newspaper or magazine. Another way to work your customers on the web is to get them involved in a dialogue with you via e-mail communication. That means building an e-mail list of highly qualified customers. To do this, you have to get them to agree to receive your periodic e-mail and encourage them to communicate back. Again, you do this by starting a dialogue. You instruct, educate, tell them what's new and ask them their opinions. You must tell customers that you are eager to have their input, and that you think their opinions are of the utmost importance to you. You must also reward them for entering a dialogue with you. Those rewards should be tangible and needed. That means offering a lot of freebies on your site, such as free reports that can be downloaded immediately. Free gifts can also be sent for and delivered. Offer discounts on purchases. Offer deals that can't be found on the street.

But merely offering something free is not good enough. We know from traditional marketing that making a free offer is not enough in itself to get people to respond. People want not only something that is free, but something free that has solid value. To wit: 'Free report tells you how to save £500 instantly on term life insurance.' Now you're offering not only a free report, but a report that will deliver a tangible benefit. A website selling property can offer a free e-manual on how to find the best deals in buying houses, and what to look for to avoid trouble. That kind of thing will build customer interest, loyalty, appreciation and repeat visits to the site to find even more helpful information.

Whatever strategy you choose to get people to be put on your e-mail list, creating such a list will be of incredible value to your business. Consider: it costs you next to nothing to send e-mails to your captured prospects. You have access to them 24 hours a day, seven days a week. You gain the opportunity to create customer relationships, and relationship marketing is one of the best marketing strategies known today.

Know the on-line market

Although the web gets more democratic every day, there are still distinctions between who you'll find on-line, and those who you find in traditional markets. People on the web tend to be:

- Better educated.
- Have more disposable income.
- Low tolerance for hard sell 'in-your-face' advertising.
- Still more males than females.
- Still younger than population average.
- More technology oriented.
- Extremely wary of scams or questionable advertising.
- Highly impatient.
- More independent thinking.
- More 'counter culture'.

But don't take anything for granted. The best approach is to find out just who is visiting your website by capturing vital points of information about all who come to visit. You do this by posting surveys, questionnaires, and other requests for information. Why should web shoppers give you this information? You'll be offering them rewards – that free stuff we talked about, for one. They don't get to download your free report until they register with their basic information. Be careful not to be demanding and threatening about asking for personal information. Make it optional! Web shoppers are highly wary, and easily chased away!

On-line marketing must be highly interactive

Internet advertising itself is different from traditional advertising in a major way: it's a two-way process. All other ads, such as newspaper ads, TV ads and radio ads, are one-way only. What the ad viewer sees is what he gets, and all decision are made at that point of contact.

But many times when shoppers read an ad, questions come to mind. With an Internet ad, those questions can be answered immediately. Better yet, the prospect can actively engage himself or herself in getting the answers they need by searching, pointing and clicking, and going deeper into your advertising messages on your webpage. The prospect can explore as deeply as the information you provide. A customer can even have a live chat with a company representative if you're set up for that.

This is an absolutely golden opportunity for a marketer!

Getting the customer involved in seeking more knowledge, asking questions, and having those queries satisfied is the road to successful selling. It's a powerful strategy because information requests are created by the shopper – not the advertiser. They initiate the communication process. That's just the opposite of cold selling! When the information seeking process starts, the customer is literally in a process of selling himself!

Make it easy for them

Since shoppers are volunteering their time and attention, it is incumbent upon you to create a website that organizes its information in a way that makes it pleasant for a customer to go deeper, and to explore. If you have designed your webpage with easy customer exploration as a goal, you'll get active, interactive customers working steadily to sell themselves on your product or service.

'Long copy' is key

This is important: on a web page, it is as vital to provide large volumes of information, as it is to include persuasive messages. Most web users are looking for facts and logic, rather than wanting to be manipulated by emotion, sex, or ego-driven desires. Most traditional advertising appeals toward the latter. But because web users tend to be better educated and readers, providing large text files filled with logical, fact-filled information, should be a very high priority.

Copy writers who write sales materials have a saying: 'Long copy outsells short copy' and 'The more you tell, the more you sell.' This means a six page sales letter will almost always out-perform a four-page sales letter, or a postcard. A large space ad with room for 200-500 words of sales copy will outsell a 25-word classified ad

...IT IS AS VITAL TO PROVIDE LARGE VOLUMES OF INFORMATION, AS IT IS TO INCLUDE PERSUASIVE MESSAGES.

almost every time. The logic of this is simple: people that are interested in your proposition will want to know as much about it as possible, they will want their questions answered and their doubts countered. They will want overwhelming testimony and proof that buying from you or going to the next step is the right, and only thing to do – and do now. Short copy just can't do this.

So here's the good news:on your web page, you have the ultimate long copy capability! It's just too expensive to send large documents of printed sales material through the mail most of the time, but a website effortlessly stores tens of thousands of words for next to nothing. The smart web-based seller will use that space to provide as much sales 'long copy' as they think necessary. You don't have to worry about overwhelming your customers because you can organize the information in such a way that they can choose to access deep information, or opt for quick overview info. The customer chooses. The more you let a customer choose, the happier they're going to be.

Furthermore, if you monitor how shoppers are accessing your information, you can learn invaluable clues about what they are interested in. For example, let's say you have an on-line furniture store. Any single item carries a number of factors upon which it can be sold – price, seating capacity, colour, make of fabric, durability, style, and so on. If you discover that shoppers select the 'style' and 'durability' categories far more than any others, you now know these are important selling points to stress. Such information can even help you plan what to emphasize in your traditional advertising.

Be wary of time distortion

If you go to Germany and travel on the Autobahn, there's no speed limit. Suddenly, driving 80 or 90 miles an hour seems normal. But when you get back to an ordinary two-way highway, where the speed limit might be 60mph, it seems like you're just crawling, even though 60 is pretty fast! It's an artificial distortion of time – purely a mental experience.

Now, remember one of the primary traits of the web shopper! They're impatient! Psychological time distortion is why. On the web, everything is 'instantly' available at the click of a mouse. In the old days, if a customer asked a question of a seller by calling or writing, they may have had to wait 24 hours, or even a week to get an answer. That kind of timeframe is not acceptable on the web! Internet surfers expect immediate gratification, and you must deliver it. This means you should have automated systems that can send information packets upon demand, or on-site locations where any question, concern or demand can be answered right now. If you fail to consider psychological time distortion in your web selling efforts, you're going to loose a lot of shoppers fast. They simply 'click-through' and they're gone!

ONE OF THE PRIMARY TRAITS OF THE WEB SHOPPER! THEY'RE IMPATIENT!

More blurred lines

Is your on-line site an advertisement – or is it a catalogue? Is it a sales letter, or an attempt at publicity? Is it persuasive copy, or is it sheer fact and logic based information?

The best answer seems to be that all these distinctions are being blurred on the web. That leaves you on uncertain ground. Should you shape your web content to look and act more like traditional advertising, or should you blend awareness creating publicity with selling? It can be tough to know exactly what your webpage is doing, even though it seems straightforward to you. What this means is that testing results is more important than ever. It also means you need to look at what others are doing to see exactly what is working and what isn't. It'll probably be a lot easier to copy a successful web seller, than find your own way later. There's nothing wrong with that. But don't forget to innovate. A website provides enormous opportunity to experiment at very little cost, other than time. When you experiment with print advertising, those failed experiments can be extremely costly. On your website, you simply delete and try again. The cost is next to nothing.

You are no longer limited by size

In one very specific way, the web is a great equalizer. A one man band operation can look as big as a mega-corporation on the web. Depending on the look of your page, there's no real way to tell the difference between a ten-person firm and a 1,000-person corporation. This is a distinct advantage for the small guys. You can compete more directly with giants by dedicating as much or more bandwidth to your page than do the bigger guys. This helps you establish a position in the market, create a brand and identity, and defeat the shopper's ability to judge you on the basis of pure size alone. Grasp this opportunity and use it to your advantage.

Keep it narrow

It's deceptively easy to lose focus on the web. Suddenly, you have all this space and power, and access to the entire global market. It's easy to go power mad! But you'll soon sober up when you start getting all kinds of traffic you're not sure what to do with. Who all are these people? Well, it's a good problem to have, and it's a very good idea to focus in on specific groups of people – find a niche. After you monitor your web activity for a while, and as you capture and break down the data, you'll start to get a feel for what you can do and who you can appeal to the most. Focus in on these highly defined groups and target them like laser beams with your marketing messages. Once you start doing a high percentage of sales to a specific group, you can branch out and go for more. Take it a little at a time. Build slowly, carefully and intelligently, with attention to detail. But also keep working to build the loyalty of those whom you connect with first. Strive hard for repeat business – even on the web, it's easier to service captured customers that you know and understand than to constantly be trying to meet the needs of new, unknown market segments.

Remain customer oriented

On the Internet, it's amazingly easy to forget that there are real people behind all those e-mails, and lists of names piling up in your database. They're not names, numbers or data – they're people with needs, desires, wants, problems and interests. Keep reminding yourself that these are people who will support your business, pay your bills and help you realize your dreams and goals in business. If you remind yourself frequently that you need these people, you'll run your website like the personalized, customer-oriented business it should be. Take each customer question and complaint seriously and resolve them in their favour. Doing so will bring you incredible loyalty, repeat business, referrals and profit.

Use a light touch

For some reason, words communicated via e-mail can seem more harsh than we intend them to be. When a person cannot look into a sincere face and see a smile, or hear a warm voice, an e-mail can easily come off as pushy and arrogant, or even unkind. This means you need to become well acquainted with Internet Etiquette, or 'Netiquette.' For example, TYPING IN ALL CAPS is viewed as SHOUTING on the Internet. You may simply want to emphasize a point, but it may not come off that way. How you word your communications is also important. You need to get the touch of writing messages that are non-threatening, warm and personal. This means heavy use of 'please' and 'thank you' and all the other linguistic pleasantries. Don't answer e-mails in abrupt sentence fragments. For example, a friend of a friend was recently trying to buy a fuel injector for a classic car. He found several dealers who had the part after a web search. He needed a little more information from one dealer before he was ready to buy. He e-mailed this:

> 'Hi, I'm interested in the fuel injector you have in stock for a Porsche 944. Can you tell me if you have the individual injector, or the injector with full rail assembly. What's the cost of the injector as a single unit, and with the full rail assembly? Can I buy either or? Thank you!'
>
> This is the answer he got back:
>
> *'It's £68 on your injector.'*

That's it! They offered no greeting, didn't really answer his question fully and ended with no sign-off, no thank you for asking, or a request for the order. No handy instructions on how to order. This blunt little message may have seemed harmless and helpful to the person who wrote it, but it certainly didn't feel that way.

Needless to say, my friends' friend didn't order from 'Mr. Blunt.' Just another sentence or two would have made all the difference.

So be careful to monitor how your messages look and feel on the screen. What you feel inside as you write does not automatically transfer to the words on the screen.

You must deliver fast and efficiently

If your website is selling products that need to be shipped, rather than downloaded immediately from the site, you need to be extra good at fulfilling orders fast. Again, the mistrust factor on the web is very high. If a first-time customer makes an order, enters in a credit card number, and then sits and waits for two weeks for something to show up on his doorstep, the suspicions which each passing day are going to burn hotter.

When you get an order, you must send an immediate e-mail confirmation to the buyer. Tell the buyer when they can expect their package to show up. Also provide a freephone number or e-mail where they can check on the progress of their order. Don't forget to say thank you.

Excellent and fast delivery is always important, but perhaps even more so, on the web. Remember the time-distortion thing we talked about. Everybody expects everything about the web to be faster, more convenient and, most of all, different!

A web marketer never rests

Your website is necessarily going to be a work in progress. Welcome to the web – where what's new today is passé tomorrow! Web pages need to be constantly reviewed. That is, you have to keep updating them, changing things and experimenting to find out what works. But also be patient enough to leave things alone long enough to fully understand what works and what does not. You must constantly monitor the competition, and observe others. When you find something that does work, leave it alone until it stops working. At the same time, push the edges. Sometimes, if it 'ain't broke, break it anyway!' I'm sorry if all this seems a little contradictory, but this is a whole new world we're talking about. Even after more than a decade of web marketing, few have figured out the basic rules of successful web marketing.

Some final suggestions

1. Before you build your web page, write an 'on-line marketing plan.' You may already have a business plan, but you'll need a new one for the web. It's a different world with different rules and unique challenges. You'll stand a much better chance of succeeding if you plan thoroughly before you put a single byte of information on-line.

2. Look for on-line alliances. One of the best ways to spread awareness about your site is to form alliances with other website owners. Get them to plug your page on their page – and include a link – in exchange for doing the same for them. Also, ask customers to place an ad for your site on their web pages. Offer them a commission on each sale that comes to you via their personal site. This is called Associate Marketing. Amazon.com is already doing this, as are many others. If you can get a couple of hundred – or a couple of thousand – people out there to help promote your site, you potentially gain all their traffic added to your own.

3. Don't forget about newsgroups and forums. Just name a subject matter, and you can bet there's a discussion group out there sharing information about it in a newsgroup, or list forum. Joining such groups can help you find new customers, and you can also post your own messages which, if you craft them carefully, can bring new traffic to your site. Be very careful! Blatant advertising in a newsgroup or list is one of the most serious breeches of Netiquette! References to your website must be extremely subtle, in context with the flow of the conversation, and must definitely not be viewed as advertising. If they are, you'll get kicked off the site, and you'll get a backlash of bad chatter about your site.

4. But newsgroups and forums are just too rich a market to ignore. Better still, they are tightly defined markets. An on-line forum for classic car enthusiasts is a guaranteed source of people interested in buying automobile related products. Match up what you sell with an on-line discussion group, and you have identified a potential gold mind of customers.

5. One more thing about this: try 'lurking.' Lurking is simply logging on to an on-line forum and reading all the postings. You'll learn a tremendous amount about what your market is thinking and talking about. You may also find many e-mail addresses of potential customers. You can contact them with a personal e-mail, which starts off as a discussion, and which can lead slowly and subtlety to a plug for your business.

6. Don't forget to advertise and promote your site off-line.

In this chapter, I have only touched on the enormous potential and challenges of Internet marketing. I urge you to dig in deeper and learn more. I am certain no one can afford to ignore the exciting power and opportunities provided by the World Wide Web, even if it only means adding support to your current bricks-and-mortar operation. Indeed, the web-based business model may be destined to be the dominant one in the near future. It's not there yet, and we need to take a serious lesson from the early dot.com disasters. But with this painful but valuable lesson behind us, we are poised to make the Brave New World of web-based marketing all it promises to be. Those who take the lead and do the best are going to get incredibly rich – no doubt about it!

6 Fast cash

Ways to boost cash when business is slow

I don't know of any business that does not hit a dead spell now and then. Suddenly, your cash flow slows down like blood flowing through an artery blocked with cholesterol! Lots of things can cause this... A downturn in the economy, a bunch of ads that didn't pull, new competition stealing your business.

Stalled cash flow is no reason for panic, but it certainly should be a motivator for you to get busy and do something about it. Indeed, a serious slow down maybe just the wake-up call you need to breathe new life into your business.

There are a lot of action plans you can implement to turn things around and jump-start cash flow. Let's look at some of the best ideas.

Fast cash 1

Bring dead inventory to life

If you've got dead inventory, you've got several problems in one. First, you have money tied up in that inventory, money you could be putting to good use. Second, you may be paying to store it. Third, the longer it sits, the more its value may fade, especially if it's a perishable or degradable product. And more.

So it makes sense to move this stuff out. That may mean slashing prices till it hurts – but if that gets the stuff moving and brings in cash, you're better off in the long run. Sometimes it's better to lose some profit in exchange for good old liquid cash, which you can use to bolster advertising, direct mail and other marketing efforts.

Another idea for dead inventory: start giving it away free! Why? Because you can tie that freebie to sales of other products. Use your dead inventory as a sales stimulus to get your entire operation going.

Now here are a dozen more creative dead inventory ideas:

1. Instead of trying to sell the stuff one item at a time, offer the whole shooting match to someone for one, low price. You eliminate inventory immediately, and get some badly needed cash. This has the added advantage of not having to advertise or spend money on direct marketing. Just make some calls, make a great deal, and unload the inventory.

    Who will buy it? Another business might. If the price is really low, how about a charity or non-profit organization? When you sell to a charity, you get some cash, and also build your image as a business with a heart. Offer your entire load to a charity or non-profit organization at one rock-bottom price.

2. How about an overseas market? With a couple of phone calls, you might be able to move the stuff to another country. What doesn't sell fast here may blaze off the shelves as an export product.

3. Trade dead inventory for advertising. Why not approach a media provider and give them your inventory in exchange for some ads? You might be able to work out a deal.

4. Look for another company that is looking for a 'free gift' idea for one of their own promotions. Give them a great deal on your dead inventory, and you'll both win. Look for a company that would be a good 'fit' for what you want to unload.

5. Barter it. Trade your dead inventory for some other kind of inventory you feel you can sell more easily.

6. Try a tandem mailing with a compatible company. Do a co-operative mailing while sharing the postal and shipping expense. The benefits of this method are many. Each company will gain the advantage of accessing the other's mailing list. If things go well, the right combination of products will stimulate sales for both of you. Both you and the other company should do better than you would with individual mailings. Advertising costs can also be shared.

7. Small lots: If your dead inventory consists of small lots of several different items, maybe your best bet would be to make connections with a person who sells at open public markets, 'crazy day' sales, car boot sales, or even flea markets. Large scale flea-marketer developers are always scavenging for items to market cheap. They'll jump at the chance to pick up your generously discounted items.

8. If you have larger stocks of discontinued items, look for a wholesaler who supplies flea-marketers, or dirt cheap bulk and

IF YOU WANT TO JUMP START CASH FLOW, GET OUT YOUR CUSTOMER LISTS AND OFFER A SPECIAL PROMOTION TO YOUR BEST CUSTOMERS.

warehouse dealers who open their doors to the general public. Don't forget large retail 'buying club' type operations. These outlets offer basement floor prices to the public, especially if they buy in large quantities. Call them up and make a deal, and get the dead weight out of your cargo hold!

9. Here's another idea using charities or other organizations looking to raise funds: print up door drop leaflets announcing fantastic discounts on a number of short stock items. Then arrange for a local charity or public organization to get volunteers to spread out and distribute your door drop leaflets. Offer the volunteer organization a percentage of the sales. Make sure your leaflets tell people this is a fundraiser and that you're being a good corporate citizen by helping out. You move dead inventory and strike a blow for your image at the same time. The leaflet could also serve as an order blank to complete the whole process at once.

10. You could also get your charity organization partners to come in and staff a bank of phones set up to take orders, and also make sales calls offering terrific deals 'for charity.' The volunteers could also handle distribution and delivery.

11. Sell the stuff to employees of other companies. Find a business with a large numbers of employees. Then make an arrangement with management to offer your inventory 'exclusively' to their employees. If you have to, cut the host company in on some profits. You may be able to move a few hundred or thousands widgets this way in just a day or two. If you tell the employees who are targeted that some of the money will go to a favourite charity, you'll boost sales even more.

12. Offer a local retailer a no-risk consignment deal. They promote the item in their ads and in their stores and you get paid only for what they actually sell. This means they don't have the risk of purchasing in advance and their advertising costs will be minimal because they can incorporate the products into their regular ads. It's an attractive deal for them, and whatever they sell will be gravy for you since you have virtually no distribution and advertising costs!

13. Auction it! Why not hold a public auction? A professional auctioneer will take care of all the details for a cut of the sales. With an auction, you may not, of course, be able to dictate a price, but you may get even more than you originally hoped! A skilled, professional auctioneer can often get more for items than you'd sell them for at discount. The auction agent will also take care of all the advertising for the big event. (Be sure to give them a list of people or businesses that you think should be notified.)

    Another advantage of an auction is that you can use the opportunity to sell things other than your dead inventory. You can sell other stuff along with it and have a very big day for cash flow! Don't forget to put a marketing message – brochure, coupon, sales piece – in the hand of every person who attends the auction!

Fast cash 2

Massage your loyal customers

If you want to jump start cash flow, get out your customer lists and offer a special promotion to your best customers.

Present this new promotion as an 'appreciation sale' for your 'exclusive supporters.' Offer a generously discounted price, but make sure you offer it only to your best, repeat customers. But as you give them a good discount, there's no reason why you can't up-sell them at the same time, or make a back-end sale! If they're your best customers, you'll have a big chance of making good sales.

When you do your appreciation sale and offer a great deal, make sure you:

- Show them in black and white what they're saving over original cost.
- Show how you're beating a competitor's price.
- Make sure they know they're the ONLY ONES getting the deal.

Fast cash 3

Now a deal for everyone else

After your special promotion to your cream of the crop customers, get out the rest of the mailing lists and send everyone some kind of lesser deal. Explain to them exactly why you are doing this. Reasons may include:

- The truth! We are doing this to bolster fast cash flow!

- Business is slow, so you, the customers benefits!

- We have just got a great one-time only buy on a bunch of stuff and we want to pass on the savings!

- We have to raise cash or lay off employees soon! Please help us keep our people employed! With your help, we can do it!

- This is the slow season and so we're offering a deal to generate cash.

- Make sure you tell them the deal will be GONE when business picks up again!

Even if the reason seem a bit negative, such as your business is in cash flow trouble, just telling it like it is can give you an honest, matter-of-fact image that customers can understand and appreciate. It's like your levelling with a friend. You're making a frank statement, and hoping for the best.

Note: some may correctly dissent on this. I know a lot of business people who wouldn't admit they were in trouble if they were down to their last nickel! The thought is that the public will see the company as a failure waiting to happen, and no one likes a loser. Yet, on the other hand, this can give many people the idea that there are great deals to be had because this company is desperate! What do you think? It's up to you to make a judgment based on how well you think you know your market.

But whatever you do, don't whine or threaten. "You must buy, or we're finished!" Remember, positive oriented marketing almost always trumps negative oriented advertising. So even if your reasons are negative, strive to couch them in a positive light.

 Fast cash 4

Sell paper

Selling paper can be a terrific cash flow remedy. What am I talking about? It's basically the opposite of 'Buy now, pay later.' What I want you to consider is a 'Pay now, get later' strategy.

The key is not to present it exactly like this, especially in these days of credit card madness, when everyone likes to 'buy now and pay later.'

Rather, think in terms of 'GET YOUR LOW RATE NOW, GET YOUR PRODUCT LATER.'

Great! But how do you get customers to 'pay now, buy later?' Let's take a look at a few ...

If you present your message right, you can convince many customers that they'll get big savings if they buy in advance and wait to get the product at a later time. Here's how you can get this done.

If you have a business that lends itself to contractual pre-selling, you can set up a special offer based on a pre-purchase discount

IMAGINE IF YOU SAID IN YOUR MARKETING MESSAGES SOMETHING LIKE THIS:

'COME IN AND BUY £20 NOTES FOR £18!'

plan. Offer an attractive discount to a customer for prepaying for a year of your services or a year's purchase of product in advance. Basically, you are offering a contract to your best customers that says they get a low price NOW, if they PAY NOW, and receive product or service later, or when they need it the most.

This strategy locks customers in for a pre-specified time frame. You get immediate cash flow.

Here's another angle on this: many smaller cities and towns, in order to encourage shopping within their own community, print their own 'money' which can only be spent in the city. For example, if the town's name is Bakersfield, the, Bakersfield Chamber of Commerce might print up 'Baker's Bucks'. These look like a cross between coupons and real currency. They can be purchased at a central location for a percentage of their face value. If a business wants to offer a 20% discount, Baker's Bucks will be available to the consumer for 80p in the pound. In other words, a customer can get £100 in Baker's Bucks for £80. Then, the Baker's Bucks cannot be used until Christmas season, or some other future date. The money comes in now, and gets redeemed later. That's immediate cash flow.

You can do the same for your business. Why not print up your own money, and tell your customers that they can buy it for 80 or 90p in the pound, and they can start spending it in 90 days, or some other time?

Call it 'Company Cash' or whatever you want.

To my knowledge, it's all perfectly legal as long as you make it clear that your company cash is not legal tender. If you don't, some scary looking government officials may want to have a word with you! Also, it's best to print your company cash in £10 denominations or larger. Printing single denomination bills makes it more difficult to get more money fast. When your customers come in with their company cash, make it easy for them to have the amount of money that matches your prices best.

Imagine if you said in your marketing messages something like this:

'Come in and buy £20 notes for £18!'

That's a gimmick that's hard to resist for the average customer. They'll gladly wait to use them later if they know they're getting a deal now, and that sometime in the future, their new money will have fantastic purchasing power in your store!

Better yet, the company cash has advantages over the contractual pre-purchase plan we mentioned first. That's because it gives the customer more flexibility. They can redeem their company cash when they're ready, and are not obligated to use it under the dictates of some pre-specified contract.

Make sure, however, you put a time limit on how long your company cash will be honoured. You don't want people coming in five years later. It's best to complete the discount process according to a carefully thought-out time frame to ensure you have the exact stock in exchange for the company cash. Targeting holidays is a great idea. You can say: 'Get Your Christmas Shopping Done In July! Buy

Discounted Company Cash Today and Spend It in December on Christmas Presents!' Linking it to a holiday period is an additional, attractive selling point.

 Fast cash 5

Gift vouchers

The Company Cash idea is really a kind of gift voucher, which brings us to another cash boosting idea: yes, the gift voucher.

I would imagine that many of you, are already selling gift vouchers, but I'm betting you're doing it in the same boring old way. You might have an advertisement or a sign posted in your store that reads: 'Gift Vouchers available.' That's nothing more than a statement of fact. It's not proactive and does nothing to motivate large numbers of people to buy a gift voucher right away. So what I want you to do is inject some real life and excitement into the idea of using gift vouchers.

Here's what I mean: why not put together a special mailing piece which you will send to your customer list. In it, explain that you realize and understand that buying gifts is a chore and a painful obligation to some people, and you have the perfect way to get all your Christmas or birthday shopping or anniversary shopping taken care of right away, and without effort. Let them know that you offer gift vouchers year-round, or say you have decided to begin offering gift vouchers now because you have never done it before.

Here's a sample letter you can send out:

Dear Preferred Customer,

Have you ever scrambled at the last minute to get your Christmas shopping done before it's too late? Have you fought your way through busy shopping malls, battled other shoppers in the store, or felt overwhelmed by your need to get your gift shopping out of the way?

Or maybe you have no idea what to get your wife, husband, or friend for their birthday, anniversary or special occasion this year?

Well, we understand how you feel. That's why we offer gift vouchers as a convenience to our best customers.

Better yet, we have chosen this non-holiday time to write to you about gift vouchers because we have a deal for you! Normally our gift vouchers sell for face value, but now for a short time, we are offering a 15% discount on gift vouchers as a special offer to you!

Also, for every £50 gift voucher you buy, we'll give you a £5 gift voucher you can treat yourself with right now! So why not get the gift-shopping monkey off your back right now and get free £5 gift vouchers to spend on yourself (or someone else).

Hurry! The offer ends in seven days! We look forward to seeing you soon!

Sincerely,
Mike Businessman

Making the gift voucher offer sweeter with a bribe is an incredibly powerful strategy. It's impossible for an offer like that to NOT get a great response! Best of all, you get cash coming in fast.

Here's another super gift voucher twist: approach a business with a large number of employees and offer to sell them a stack of gift vouchers they can hand out to their employees next Christmas at bonus time. Many companies offer year-end or holiday bonuses anyway. You can cash in now by letting the company get this task behind them buy purchasing gift vouchers from you at a discount. This can be an amazingly easy way to make a few hundred, or a few thousand sales in a single day, and get an injection of cash flow that may solve all your capital needs instantly.

Selling paper in the forms of contract pre-purchase discounts, company cash, or gift vouchers is a fast way to generate cash flow. Try, but be careful. Be sure to keep your future fulfilment costs in mind. When the paper starts coming in to redeem purchases, you must have the stock on hand to complete the deal.

 Fast cash 6

The 'preferred customer' strategy

Creating a 'Preferred Customer's Club' is an excellent paper sales strategy that gets cash flowing fast.

Here's how you do it

Choose your best customers from your customer lists and send them a letter telling them that they have been selected to be members

IF YOU REALLY NEED CASH NOW, YOU MAY HAVE TO DO SOMETHING YOU DON'T LIKE.

of your exclusive Preferred Customer's Club, and they will enjoy special 'membership only' benefits that will include:

- First notification of introductory items which they can buy at a discount.

- Advance notification of all special deals.

- The opportunity to buy close-outs and short stock items at a huge savings not offered to 'ordinary' customers.

- Credit deals not available to others.

- A personalized discount card.

- Free subscription to your customer newsletter which will contain discount coupons, etc.

- Only they will receive notification of unadvertised sales.

- Any other benefits you think may be appropriate.

Now, here comes the fast money part. To join the Preferred Customer's Club, they pay a membership fee. Make sure you let them know the fee will be more than made up for in discounts and buying advantages. If you make the fee £20, for example, and you sell 500 preferred customer memberships, that £10,000 fast!

This is one of the ultimate paper selling strategies because you not only get money upfront, but you don't actually have to tie it to a specific product, as you do with paper money or gift vouchers.

Rather, membership privileges are general and ongoing. They get discounts and benefits, but not specific products, in return for the paper (membership) they buy. The beauty of this is the ease of fulfilment. Future fulfilment costs will be minimal—a few extra mailings, some discounts, and such. But if you're a savvy marketer, you'll have your eye on the back-end and up-selling as your preferred customer's come in for their special deals. That way you can more than make up for what you give away in bolstered sales.

Fast cash 7

A cash boosting strategy that hurts but works

If you really need cash now, you may have to do something you don't like. One such idea is to go to your customers who have outstanding debts, and offer them a discount if they'll pay right away. For example, if a customer owes you £250, tell them it's only £225 if they pay right away. Yes, you lose money, but you also get money in the pocket fast. Really, it's no different to taking out a loan. You borrow £1,000 but you pay back £1,100. What you're doing here is your own invoice discounting. Many companies today specialize in purchasing invoices at a discount for a fee. But you can do it yourself by calling in your debts now for a discount.

The idea does have some advantages, however. You may collect debts that never would have been paid otherwise. Also, carrying a customer's debt erodes its value the longer it remains unpaid. Another slight advantage is that you earn the goodwill of the customer if you are careful to let them know you are helping them out with your discount offer. This can only bolster future sales. And don't forget to try to make another sale at the same time you offer a discount on debt. A back-end sale makes up for anything you lose on a discount.

Remember – slow business and cash crunches happen! You wouldn't be doing business right if they didn't. They key is to find strategies to bolster cash flow when you really need to. There's nothing worse than inaction. When you think creatively, you can move out dead inventory, revitalize cash flow, and turn things around faster than you ever thought possible. Losers see problems as problems. Winners see problems as opportunities. Dead inventory and stalled cash flow may be just the very thing you need to electrify your business!

7

112 brainstorm marketing ideas for your business

 Brainstorm 1

CD-ROM catalogues

Is your catalogue getting into your customers' hands, but more and more remaining unopened? Maybe it's time to put some excitement into it by stamping your catalogue onto CD-ROM. You'll increase sales appeal. Also, CD catalogues can be targeted and easily personalized for each client. CD-ROM enables you to do what no paper catalogue could ever do – use moving pictures, animation, sound, and full-colour, mind-blowing special effects. Based on what you know about your customer's buying habits, each CD can be programmed to appeal to those individual habits.

A CD can also be programmed to interact live with the Internet. It can send customers to your site, and recognize them when they get there. Customers can also take advantage of special offers and custom designed discounts you've placed on each disc. You can take advantage of how easy a CD-ROM can automatically track results when the customer visits the website via your disc.

And there's still more: your repeat CD catalogue customers can give you a wealth of data about their tastes in music, their preferences in sports, favourite reading materials, their sizes in clothing and the styles they love, and much more. For example, when customers see clothing in their sizes and favourite styles displayed on 'virtual models', they'll know you've got exactly what they want. CD-ROM discs speak directly to customers by name ... and then display lead-ins that highlight the kind of products they're most likely to buy, based on past purchasing patterns.

CD-ROM catalogues can be custom-tailored to match national, regional, or local interests. If you want, you can target your efforts to any combination of demographics, including income, age, gender, and any other categorization that applies to your products.

If you sell by catalogue, or even if you don't, get yourself to a CD-ROM expert right now and make your catalogue a CD-ROM catalogue – it's an entirely new dimension of selling that's destined to leave the old way of doing things in the dust sooner than later.

 Brainstorm 2

On-line catalogues

The publication *Catalog Age* conducted a study which showed that as of 1997, 73% of all catalogue companies have put their catalogues on-line. Not all of them have been successful. Lee Jeans, for example, after pouring huge amounts of money into selling jeans on-line, recently pulled the plug on their on-line catalogue until 'further notice.'

Yet, many on-line catalogues are doing well. Consumer confidence in online shopping is increasing as security issues are addressed.

People need to feel safe using their credit card numbers on-line. The successful on-line catalogue must do all it can to reassure shoppers that keying in a credit card number, and other personal information is 110% safe!

On-line catalogues are a new way to reach existing and new markets. They cost relatively little to establish. They can leverage existing databases, processes, and marketing techniques. Anything that can be sold through mail-order can be sold on-line.

Another reason to establish an online catalogue is the fact that your competitors are already doing it!

Here are my Top Six Tips for Successful On-line Selling:

1. Get to know the web well first by becoming a frequent Web surfer. If you're going to be involved with building an on-line catalogue, you must know the playing field well, and be comfortable there.

2. Understand that the web is its own unique marketing and sales medium. That means using a pull method to get customers to your on-line catalogue, rather than a push method.

3. Your on-line catalogue will be a two-way communication medium. Use it to build relationships with customers.

4. Don't be static. Create a useful, informational, interactive and well-organized Web 'experience.' Your on-line catalogue should not be merely an electronic version of your paper catalogue. Interesting content, interactivity, easy navigation, and a solid, secure, on-line shopping process is a must.

5. Your sales, service, marketing and fulfilment processes and systems will need to be modified to serve the web customer.

6. Test everything! Conduct a testing period with a limited number of customers for usability, impression, understanding content, and for making sure things are functioning properly before you go big time and spend a lot of money.

Brainstorm 3

Placemats in restaurants

I like the idea of advertising on placemats in restaurants. They get looked at by people waiting to eat. They get looked at when two people are on a date and they run out of conversation. They might as well be looking at your ad. Placemat ads probably work best for businesses with an affinity to restaurants, such as cinemas, theatres, entertainment venues, such as bowling alleys or night clubs. If people are out to eat, they may be up for other activities as well. Can you sell insurance on a placemat? Well, an insurance agent's toll free number and a catchy plug might pull some response – it depends on the kind of restaurant. Consider what kind of restaurant will be using placemats with ads on them – will a fancy, fine dining establishment be using them? Not likely! More likely, paper placemats are for everyday restaurants that serve the common crowd. So are they a good place to sell a luxury car, or diamonds? Maybe, but not likely. The only true way to find out if they'll work for you is a test. You'll know a lot more after you try. But it might be a better idea to ask others how they did with their placemat ads before you risk some of your own money.

 Brainstorm 4

Personal letters

If you want to almost guarantee your direct mail piece gets opened, then hand lettering the address will do the job for you. It's a world of difference over a printed label address that just screams out 'junk mail!' But how do you get so many thousands of envelopes hand addressed? You hire people to do it. It won't cost you that much, and the results will speak for themselves.

What about making the whole letter personal? Well, it's not a good idea to hand-write an entire letter. That's just not feasible on any scale. You're going to have to type your letter, but you can sign it with your personal signature.

When we're talking about personal letters for the purposes of marketing, we're more likely talking about consultants or professionals looking for small numbers of individual clients. But it's well worth their while to sit down and write personal letters to potential clients. If you put aside a day or two, you can write a lot of letters to potential clients and net some new business. A personal letter to a potential customer is going the extra mile to make a connection with a future customer. Your letter should always be followed up with a phone call. Doing so will increase successful response by 300% or more. That's why it's worthwhile to write personal letters and follow-up with a one-on-one phone call, or even a personal visit.

Brainstorm 5

Inbound telemarketing

Each and every call that comes into your business has value. You must realize this and make it part of your company philosophy. Every call is not only an opportunity to make a sale, but it can also tell you a great deal about what's going on with your marketing effort.

For example, your inbound calls can help you determine your marketing costs. If you spend £10,000 monthly on advertising, and get about 1,000 calls, each call costs you £10. Are you getting £10 of value back on each of those calls? Are your average sales enough to overcome £10 per call? Let your employees know the value of each call – they'll treat each phone call like it was a £10 bill to be lost or gained.

Increase your inbound sales success by rewarding your employees for good performance. For example, consider creating a 'Phone Star Award' to the employee who gets the full contact information of the most inbound callers. At sales meetings, make a big deal out of presenting the award, and give the employee a free weekend at a spa, or money, or anything of value.

Good inbound phone performance can only come from good training. Your employees must know what to do, and what goals you are shooting for when they take an incoming call.

INCREASE YOUR INBOUND SALES SUCCESS BY REWARDING YOUR EMPLOYEES FOR GOOD PERFORMANCE.

Getting information is as important as making sales. When your employees take incoming calls, make sure they:

1. Ask if the caller is a prior customer. If the answer is yes, then have them say something like, "We are updating our customer list. Would you mind giving me your address and phone number so that we can update our records?

2. If the caller says they are not a prior customer have your employees say something like: "I'd like to send you a free report that you'll find very interesting. It will help you … If you give me your address I'll send it out to you today."

3. Get an e-mail address from each incoming call. Offer the customer a free gift that can be sent by e-mail and then ask for the e-mail address. Your gift can be an electronic coupon, an informational report, a screen saver, or anything you can think of.

Get the most out of your incoming calls – that means making sales, or gathering prospect information for later use.

Brainstorm 6

Outgoing calls

Cold calling is hard work, but warm calling makes sales happen. Thus, your challenge for outgoing calls is to make them "warm" before you call them. One great way to do that is to send a direct mail piece to a prospect first, and then call them and ask about, "the free report I sent you three days ago" or the "newspaper article I sent you." If you want to go the extra mile, call them first and tell them you're sending them something. Then send it, then call back. You'll have a thoroughly warmed up prospect!

Always get the first name of a prospect, or have it before you call. Call them by their name, and if you can, tell them you were referred to them by a person they know. You get that name by asking each caller for a person they know whom you can call next.

Use open-ended questions when you call a prospect. That means asking questions that start with why, what, or tell me... For example, "Tell me what you think about life insurance, and if you think it's a good thing to have?" This way you get the prospect selling himself!

Make sure you listen and wait for a customer response. A good benchmark is to let the customer do 80% of the talking, while you do 20%. That's right! Let the customer sell himself –let it happen and it will! Don't be afraid of dead space. You don't have to fill every minute of the sales call with your chatter. It's always better to listen, then respond to what the prospect tells you.

Be listening for a problem that is causing your prospect trouble or pain, then try to understand it, and repeat it back to him or her.

Then tell how your product will solve the problem or eliminate the pain. When you do that, you get a sale more often than not.

If appropriate, always ask each incoming caller for an appointment so you can meet with them person-to-person.

Always make the most of each outgoing call, and always have a specific reason to call! Know what you are doing, and be well-prepared long before you pick up the phone!

 Brainstorm 7

Matchbook advertising

Soon after the matchbook was invented in 1889 by Joshua Pusey, the Mendelson Opera Company used the new 'flexible' match as an advertising vehicle. It was a tremendous success. By 1900, the matchbook was in wide use as an effective, promotional vehicle. The advantages of matchbook ads are many: selectivity, flexibility, frequency, low cost, and the ability to supplement your other advertising efforts. They do have some disadvantages, however. The drawbacks are the perception that they are 'junk ads,' and the high numbers of other companies using matchbooks, creating saturation. Your best bet is to test matchbook ads to see if they work for you. I don't think they can be simply dismissed as a second-rate advertising vehicle. For example, the Royal Family issued memorabilia matchbooks of Charles and Diana's wedding. That's high class! Today, they're valued collector's items. Speaking of collecting, matchbooks are a hot collector's item. If you issue your own matchbook cover design, you may get some extra mileage by being listed in collector's catalogues and on collectors' web pages!

Brainstorm 8

Breakfast seminars

If you're going to conduct a seminar, consider a breakfast seminar. The early morning hours are when you'll get people at their best, most optimistic, most willing to pay attention and learn. A breakfast seminar on Monday morning is even better. People jump at a chance to start their work week with something different. Also, breakfast tends to be the cheapest meal of the day. So over a plate of eggs and some good coffee, you'll have a bright, cheerful attentive audience glad to be there, feeling aggressive about starting a new week. Breakfast seminars work best for the bosses – those that can make their own schedules and arrange their calendars accordingly. And when you get these people, you get the movers and shakers – the people that can make decisions, and make something happen. It's a golden opportunity for you to make connections with the people you most need to connect with. The result can be new business, joint ventures, co-op advertising opportunities and more.

 Brainstorm 9

Private unveilings

If you're getting ready to bring out a new product, you may want to consider making the event an exclusive, private affair, inviting only those people who can make things happen for you. You're going to reveal your new item to the world sooner or later, but why not create some buzz and add a little drama to the event? Such an event is especially enticing to the press. If you want some free media

PEOPLE JUMP AT A CHANCE TO START THEIR WORK WEEK WITH SOMETHING DIFFERENT.

coverage, conduct an exclusive, private event – and tell the press you're willing to let them in the back door! Tell your press contact that they can be the first to get a line on your latest thing, and that there will also be other important people they can gain access too. Sometimes a little showman-ship can go a long way in free media coverage, and also gets a word of mouth buzz going on the street. When that happens, you may find dozens of people lining up to be the first to get your new item so they can have the bragging rights – and tell others about it. That's the kind of word of mouth you want to generate!

 Brainstorm 10

Previews

Giving the public a preview of something new is a well-known way to generate free publicity and street buzz. Very often you'll see cinemas offering a midnight preview of a new film, and only in key, selected cities. In truth, they want as many people to see the film as possible, but the preview intrigues the press and other people as well. The result is increased curiosity and demand to see the film. A preview also whets the appetite for the product. In Japan, it's

SOMETIMES YOU MUST LOSE MONEY ON YOUR FIRST SALE, SO YOU CAN MAKE MONEY ON THE NEXT

common knowledge among business folks there that the anticipation of a new product is almost as important as getting the product itself. For example, a Japanese bicycle company builds bikes that are custom designed to meet the physical dimensions of each rider. The customer is first scanned by a computer which calculates the perfect bicycle frame for the body type. The bicycle can be built on the spot, but the company requires the customer wait two weeks to receive it. Why? Because they know that the anticipation of the customer is as important as getting the product itself! A preview can bring this same desire-producing anticipation. A preview is also a chance to test market your product and get early response. If you get negative feedback, you still have a chance to make things right before you release the product for general sales.

 Brainstorm 11

Personalized letters

Now, more than ever, direct mail letters can be easily personalized by computer. That means not starting out with 'Dear Friend' but 'Dear Bob Jones,' or just 'Dear Bob.' Yes, consumers are already used to this, and they know computers are doing all the work. But it still has an effect that's much better than an anonymous greeting. Even if computerized personalizing is industry standard, you at least need to be up to that industry standard! Remember, the best direct mail sales letters should look as little like a sales letter as possible, and as much like a personal letter from a friend as possible. You can also personalize letters beyond the name. You can also make reference to the town a person lives in within your letter, and even discuss something you know they already own. You get this kind of information from your customer database. Thus, the more information you store in your database, the more you can personalize your letters. You can also find out more about your list by conducting surveys, using contests to gather information and using your order forms to get additional information. The bottom line is, the more you personalize, the stronger you make your sales letter.

 Brainstorm 12

Loss leaders

Sometimes you have to give to receive. In selling, sometimes you must lose money on your first sale, so you can make money on the next, and the sale after that. Many marketers, especially new, green marketers, have a difficult time with not making a big profit on their first sale. But those with the long-view in mind realize that single sales rarely make anyone rich – it's those strings of sales that really get the money ball rolling. When you offer a fantastic product at an unbelievable price, you get a great response, and hundreds and thousands of unbelievably valuable customer names for your list. You may break even, or even lose money on that terrific offer. But the list you gain can be used to go after literally dozens of repeat sales. Each name on your list has a lifetime value – the amount of purchases each name makes over a period of months or years, or for as long as they remain your customer. When you keep this enormous value in mind, the loss leader starts to make a lot more sense. I'm not saying you should try to lose money on your lead product – the more you make the better. But if your response is poor, you're losing a lot of future value you could be developing for your own future. Smart marketers build the loss of their loss leader into their overall budget. Yes, there's always an element of risk. Your upfront loss can end up being a total loss, but more often than not, you gain in the long run when you keep you eye on the future, and plan to make multiple sales, rather than just one.

 Brainstorm 13

House to house canvassing

If you want to deep market a geographic area, and do it with a fine-toothed comb, house to house canvassing is one way to get it done. Many sellers turn ice cold at the thought of going home to home to sell, or do anything else. But many of the best sellers don't shy away from house to house work, especially in down time, or on evenings or weekends. Going house to house is a great way to gather names for your customer list, and gather additional information about each person. Tell people you are conducting marketing research, and then ask them the questions you need to know to sell them in the future. You'll get a better response if you offer something for their time, such as a free gift, or a discount coupon on something you sell. When you go back a second time, you are no longer making a cold call. The person already knows you, and if they like you, you're going to make sales.

Going house to house is slow work, but you can speed things up by enlisting help. A terrific source of free help is colleges and universities. Place an ad in a campus newspaper offering 'internships' and on-the-job work experience to marketing students. They fan out to do your leg work, and you give them a strong letter of recommendation for the day they graduate and need a real job in the world of business.

I think too many sellers spend too much time on paperwork or non-selling bureaucracy when they could be out selling door to door. Get the paperwork done at the weekend or at night. But during prime selling time, go door to door and work on your sales pitch. The worst that can happen is that you'll learn what not to do in selling, and the best that can happen is that you'll make a lot of extra sales.

 Brainstorm 14

Supermarket boards

Just about everybody goes to the supermarket now and then. Better yet, the person who goes to the supermarket most often is very likely to be the person who makes all the buying decision for the family. In supermarkets you'll find bulletin boards cluttered with hundreds of postings. The good thing about this board is that it's a venue for free advertising for you. The bad thing is all the clutter. If you're lucky, you'll find a spare patch of board that is not covered

A TERRIFIC SOURCE OF FREE HELP IS COLLEGES AND UNIVERSITIES.

by some other scrap of paper with the picture of a lost pet or an old car for sale.

So the challenge is to stand out, like it is with so much other advertising. Your advantage is that your posting will not be just another amateurish attempt to sell a '92 Ford with low mileage! You are going to post a vivid sign with an attention grabbing headline that will make people stop and look further, as beneath your headline will be compelling sales copy. Beneath that a freephone number in large print. You will also include a pocket of take-ones with your complete contact information on it. Stapled to each take-one will be your business card.

After you post your piece, stand back and look at the board from a distance. Does your posting leap out from the pack and attract attention? If not, it's time to make changes until it does stand out. Don't forget to conduct a test of your supermarket board ad. If it brings no results, you need to go back to the drawing board and find something that works. But once you get a board ad that works, it's time to get them up in every supermarket board, and other public bulletin boards in the region. If you're going to use public bulletin boards, do it all the way, do it right, and don't stop testing until you make it pull results.

 Brainstorm 15

Point of sales advertising

This innovative form of advertising has produced some wonderful results. What is it? It's anything at the point of sale that attracts customers and makes it easier for people to buy. Point of purchase ads come in many forms, including moving and unmoving varieties. This can include everything from flip cards to interactive auto-mated displays.

Studies show an 88% average gain above normal sales when a product is on the shelf and point of purchase advertising is used. That's because studies show that 70% of buying decisions are made in the store. A point of purchase ad bolsters the chance a sale will be made – by 88%. That's fantastic.

And listen to this: in a study done for *POP Times,* an in-store display combined with a 15% price reduction boosted sales by 279%! Even more exciting, the combined effect of a discount, advertising feature, in-store display and feature/display mix increased average sales by 545%!

So are you interested in point of purchase advertising? Just repeat to yourself: "545% increase in sales ... 545% increase in sales..."

 Brainstorm 16

Cross promotions/selling

Here's a great example of cross marketing: a man by the name of Sanford Ziff founded a business he called Sunglasses Hut. At the time, most sunglasses were worn by older adults, and most were sold by opticians. (Hard to believe now, isn't it!). But Ziff used cross marketing by setting up sunglasses 'huts' in the middle of shopping malls where a lot of young people could be found. He also set up on college campuses, and in sporting goods stores. Suddenly, young people everywhere wouldn't be caught dead without a cool pair of shades!

Malls, campuses and sporting goods stores – all examples of cross promotion because prior to that, sunglasses were sold mostly by opticians. It doesn't seem like cross promotion now, but that's just a testament to how well it worked!

How can you cross promote your product? Only your imagination is the limit. What other business, location, or venue can find a new market, a new angle for what you sell? Think again of Sanford Ziff. He saw the potential market, and went to where that market was. You can do the same.

 Brainstorm 17

Workshops

I have a friend who is a freelance writer and media consultant. From time to time he puts on a workshop for business people. He calls it: *How to Write Press Releases and Get Free Media Coverage*. He limits enrolment to 12 people. The charge is £50 per person. He spends an afternoon explaining the art of writing press releases. He doesn't just talk. He makes them work! He requires each participant to write at least two press releases, and then he gives them each a one-on-one critique. He sends them home with some model press releases and a format they can use to write future releases. I said: "That's a nice way to make £600 for an afternoon's work." He agreed, but then added: "I don't do it for the £600. I do it for the business it generates for me." Explaining, he said at least one, and sometimes several of the workshop members inevitably come back to hire him for writing projects: business plans, company year-end reports, grant writing, advertising copy, direct mail pieces, and even press releases. "I don't think I've ever generated less than £10,000 in new business every time I put on my little workshop."

Think about that. This man gets PAID £600 to get thousands of pounds in future business! He doesn't PAY £600 for an ad – he COLLECTS £600 to get all the business he can handle! Indeed, he never gives his workshop more than once a year. That would generate more customers than he could ever serve!

Does this give you an idea about what a workshop can do for your business? Workshops can work for not only a professional consultant like Ken, but can work for any business. The owner of a hobby shop can conduct a workshop on kite building or model rocketry. The owner of a sporting goods store can give a workshop on fly fishing. A health food store owner can conduct a workshop on vegetarian cooking. It's fun, it generates new clients, and brings people back to your place of business for sales!

So try a workshop. It's simply a fantastic way to generate new business!

 Brainstorm 18

Bag stuffers

When you bag up your customer's purchases, don't miss an opportunity to slip marketing materials along with everything else. You know customers are going to look into the bag – that's a prime goal of direct marketing – getting them to look! Print up flyers, ad sheets, brochures, or just about anything with a great offer on it. Don't forget a discount coupon. Nothing will get them to come back faster than a coupon they can bring in for savings. You can also place a free gift in the bag. This has the powerful 'I never expected to get something extra' impact that works so well to make customers adore you and come back for more. A free item can also double as an advertising vehicle – a T-shirt with your logo on it, a pen with your name and number on it, a cup with your info on it – and lots of other stuff you can think of on your own. Just remember, customers are going to look in that bag. Give them something to find, and bag more sales!

 Brainstorm 19

Direct sales people

What if you could command a small army of sales people to spread out across the land to sell your products for you – and better still, what if this small army would not cost you a single penny to build? All they do is bring you money and business. Getting others to sell for you – on a commission basis – is one of the most powerful selling strategies I can think of. Take out an ad seeking sales people. Tell them what their potential earning is on your product, what their commission is and how much they can make per year. The more they sell for you, the more they make. Screen your applicants well. You want only the best people representing your company. Most of your applicants won't make the cut, but one good seller will have the value of 100 poor sellers. Provide excellent training. Infect your sellers with the energy and spirit of your company. Make their commission generous, and offer special incentives for reaching high sales goals. There's no reason why you shouldn't take out an ad today and get other people selling for you as soon as possible. It will cost you next to nothing, and your new army of direct sales people can double, triple or totally explode your sales numbers in just weeks!

REMEMBER, A SIGN REPRESENTS YOU AND YOUR BUSINESS. IT MUST LOOK GOOD!

 Brainstorm 20

Signs

Signs come in many manifestations. They can include huge bill-boards on a road, or the small sign you tape up on your store front window. The most important thing a sign must do is capture attention, be seen, and then deliver information people can act upon. Don't make a 'do nothing' sign that carries only your name and location. Go further by making an offer, urging people to come to your location to buy. Give them a reason to come. 'Free coffee or beverage with every meal!' 'Come in for a test drive and get free gas!' '50% off everything – today only!' One of the best kinds of signs is those you can change the lettering on whenever you want, or can be programmed to flash your message of the day. Signs go out to where the public is, so work hard to find where your best clients are likely to be located and place your sign there. It's similar to finding the right section of the newspaper for your ad, or the right magazine by subject. Remember, a sign represents you and your business. It must look good! Your signs should also follow the theme of all your marketing tools: use the same colour and design elements that grace your business cards, your ads, your product packaging, your product itself. This way, your sign will benefit from the cumulative effort of all your marketing tools.

Brainstorm 21

Banner signs

Perhaps thousands of people pass by your business location every day. They've seen it so often you're all but invisible. But one way to wake people up and make them look is to make a brightly lettered, large banner and drape it across the front of your building on special days. Now people will notice because they see something different. A banner has a festive "special' effect that tells passers-by that something different is going on at your store today. What that special event might be is up to you. But if you want to shake things up and get people to look, try a bright banner sign outside your store – and make it say something interesting and compelling. 'Year-end stock clearance sale!' 'Your birthday today! Stop in for a free drink!' 'No deal turned down today – just try us!'

 Brainstorm 22

Centres of influence

Sociologists have a term for people who are always the first to try new things, and who naturally lead the way in their cities, neighbourhoods and rural communities. They call them 'early adopters.' They are the people everyone else watches. If they try something new, and it works, everyone else follows along. For example, if an early adopter farmer decides to plant a new variety of corn, before long, every other farmer in the county is planting it as well. They didn't want to take the risk themselves, but when the early adopter went ahead, they felt comfortable doing it themselves.

I call these kind of people 'centres of influence.' They're the people who have the natural power to make others follow their leads. In your sales efforts, finding people who are centres of influence can help you multiply your sales many times. When you sell your product to such a person, sometimes all you have to do is say that 'So-and-so bought one from me yesterday.' If 'so-and-so' is a centre of influence, the prospect in front of you is going to feel much more comfortable about buying.

A centre of influence is also a terrific referral source. Find a person that others respect and listen to, and get that person to recommend you, and you'll get dozens of new sales fast.

How do you find a centre of influence? It's a matter of asking around, talking to people, and listening. You'll be surprised at how certain names come up again and again as that community's 'early adopter' or 'centre of influence.'

 Brainstorm 23

Gift baskets

A free gift is a great marketing tool, and a gift basket is more of the same, except stronger and better! Everyone likes to get something for free from a business, but an entire gift basket has an even stronger impact. Before you start worrying about cost, your gift basket does not have to cost appreciably more than a single free gift, it just needs to have the perception of costing more. You can fill a gift basket with a large number of very inexpensive items. With a gift basket, people don't see quality, they see quantity. Gift baskets are excellent for holidays and special promotions. Better still, when you advertise a 'free gift basket' that sounds better than just a 'free gift.' The increased advertising pull alone can make up for any extra cost you may have to put into developing your gift basket.

 Brainstorm 24

Invitation only events

Sometimes businesses put on 'unadvertised sales' and I think it's a terrific idea. It's an invitation only event. The only people who get to take part in such a sale are preferred customers – those who have a track record of buying a lot. They are informed by personal letter or even phone call. It's all part of a larger strategy to massage a customer list for more profits. By focusing on premium customers, businesses squeeze even more money and sales out of them by making them feel special, by offering them exclusive shopping privileges, and inviting them to sales events no one else gets to attend. By giving extra special attention to select customers, you build their loyalty and keep them coming back. They also spend more money than other customers. You can afford to put more time and resources into such customers because each may have the value of 10 or 20 'ordinary' customers. It's a truth of business that 80% of your business comes from 20% of your customers. With this in mind, it only makes sense to treat that highly valuable 20% like they are special to you – because they are!

Brainstorm 25

On-vehicle advertising

Your vehicle can be a travelling billboard for your business. A magnet sign on your vehicle, or having your message painted directly on your vehicle is like getting a free ad every time you drive your car, van or truck. Broad-sided vehicles like trucks and vans can blast exciting, high-visibility, high impact messages to the public. Make sure you put your freephone number on your vehicle, and even your web page address. Simply putting your company name on your vehicle is not enough. All that says is 'This is me.' It does nothing to prompt action. Get your phone number, address, and even a picture of your product on the vehicle, too. If you're going to use your vehicle for advertising, make the most of it.

 Brainstorm 26

Per enquiry ads

If you're strapped for advertising funds, consider a per-inquiry ad (PIA) agreement with an advertising provider. With such a deal, you pay only for the paid responses an ad generates. If the ad flops completely, you pay nothing. If it's a success, you pay for only what the ad brought in. You can arrange a PIA with just about any medium, from newspaper to TV. Many will not accept such an offer, but others will. You don't know until you ask. If you are a first-time advertiser, you have a better chance. The media source may agree to a PIA to win your future business. A second-best arrangement is a 'per response' ad. In this situation, you pay for every response whether a sale is made or not. It's still a pretty good deal. You may have to pay more to get an ad outlet to agree to a PIA, but it's still an excellent deal if you can get it.

 Brainstorm 27

Public speaking

Giving a public speech is similar to conducting your own seminar, but is less formal. A seminar more often involves a specific learning process, handouts, workshops and more. But a public talk is simply you saying something interesting to an audience of listeners. Yet, such an event still has all the advantages of a full-blown seminar. It's a chance to reach new customers, position yourself as an expert, and capture names for your customer list. You can either put on your own speeches, or get invited to speak at other groups' events. Contact a local speaker's bureau and sign up. You can also promote and advertise your own public lecture. Make sure you invite the media to get a chance at free ink or air time. If you can get paid for a public lecture, all the better. That way you get paid to push your product and gather in new customers. Free lectures will pull a better response, but paid lectures can work just as well if your topic is hot and timely.

POSTERS MAKE EXCELLENT FREE GIFTS.

Brainstorm 28

Posters

There are many ways to use posters to advertise and get attention for your business. Here are some of the best ideas:

- Take a photograph of your product and have it made into a poster. Distribute the poster throughout town. Don't forget to include your freephone number and some copy to tell the poster viewer where to get the product, and what it will do for them.

- Posters make excellent free gifts.

- If you get some free media, blow up a picture and the article and make a poster out of it. Put it up in your place of business for everyone else to see.

- Use them on your stand and booths at trade shows, flea markets and fairs.

- Print sales copy on the back and use them as a direct mail vehicle.

- Place helpful information on your poster, such as emergency numbers, the schedule for local ball games, or theatre dates.

- Use them as ceiling hangers.

- Put them on or near public bulletin boards.

- If you make them artistic and pleasing to look at, give them away and gets ads posted up in offices and homes all over your selling area.

Brainstorm 29

Postcards

Postcard mailings are an excellent direct marketing vehicle with many advantages. First, they are less expensive to mail than sales letters in envelopes. Postcards are in-your-face advertising because they don't have to be opened. People cannot help but look at them, even as they throw them away. Postcards work extremely well as a follow-up mailer to those who did not respond to your first sales letter mailing. Postcards can have bright, attention grabbing, full-colour pictures on one side and your sales copy on the other side. Postcards can be used to say thank you, to carry a discount coupon, to announce a sale or a new location, and more.

Studies show that 'junk postcards' get read with much higher rates than do direct mail pieces in envelopes. Also, oversized postcards pull better response than smaller postcards.

 Brainstorm 30

Cinema ads

When you watch television, you expect to see commercials. Even if you don't like them, you realise they pay for the programming you watch for free. But when you go to a cinema, you pay to see the movie. You also buy vastly overpriced popcorn and beverages. Then, on top of that, when you settle into your seat, the cinema obligates you to watch ads. That doesn't seem fair – now you're paying for the privilege to see someone's ads. This is probably part of the reason that cinema ads do not work very well. They are perhaps the poorest performing ads of any kind. Another reason they don't work is that when people are in a dark cinema, they are not likely to grab a pen and write down a freephone number they see on the screen. They just want the movie to start so they can enjoy themselves. So, in general, I don't recommend cinema ads. They just don't work very well for most products and services. Perhaps what they work best for is to advertise upcoming concerts and other entertainment venues. If people pay to go see a movie, they will pay to go see a concert. Cinema ads do reach a captive audience and force the viewer to confront your pitch, but the effect may backfire because of the irritation factor. Go ahead and test some cinema ads if you want to, but put your resources elsewhere first.

 Brainstorm 31

Classified ads

The good old classified ad is a great friend to the seller. I wonder how many business empires were launched with a single classified ad? Many, I'm sure! Classified ads are inexpensive, and if used right, can lead to customers, sales and profits. The biggest mistake most beginners make is trying to make a classified ad do too much. It's difficult indeed to sell a high-priced or even moderately priced item directly with a classified ad. Rather, a classified ad works better as a lead generator. Using it in a two-step approach is best. That means offering something free or enticing and getting prospects to respond and seek more information. When they do respond, you send them your full-length marketing tool, such as a sales letter, audio tape, video tape, or direct them to your web page. A classified ad is also an excellent vehicle to advertise your freephone number. With a classified, you have just a precious few words to get attention, raise interest and desire, and prompt action. The best classified ads offer something valuable and free. They also promise a benefit, and they work even better if you put a time limit on how long your terrific offer will be available. The classified ad is a superb tool to test an idea or product before you buy a bigger ad. It's important to choose the proper publication in which to run your classified ad: match the publication subject with your product.

 Brainstorm 32

Radio ads

Radio advertising is an intrusive kind of advertising – it forces its way into the listener's mind. It also has tremendous reach and market penetration. Radio ads go wherever a radio goes, and radios are everywhere: in cars, on the beach, in bedrooms, in the garage, even in people's ears while they jog. Radio ads inform, educate, entertain, get attention, and can easily be targeted to specific audiences. Radio can keep your name in front of your customer's mind so they won't forget you. Perhaps the greatest strength of radio is the fact that it employs the 'theatre of the mind' – it makes the listener create images inside the mind based on what he hears on the radio.

There are two broad ways to make use of radio advertising:

1. Institutional advertising

This involves messages telling who you are, what you do, where you are located and why it would benefit shoppers to come in.

2. Saturation advertising

These are those special times when you are getting ready for a big push, such as a grand opening or a big sale. You buy up as much time as you can for two or three days and have your ads run every hour of the day. You try to reach as many listeners as possible as they come and go and turn their radios on and off throughout the day. In this case you may use up to three months worth of your advertising budget in just a couple of days, so plan carefully.

Here are my Top 11 Radio Ad Tips

1. Use a station you know your customers listen to. Teens listen to rock, older adults choose classical or talk radio, and so on. But you should also conduct a survey among your customer list to find out which stations they listen to the most.

2. News time is the best time to advertise. People pay attention to, and listen more closely to, radio news. It costs more, but you'll get what you pay for.

3. Use radio when you want to pinpoint a specific target market. Radio does this better than print or TV.

4. Studies show radio works best for restaurants and supermarkets. Next in line in terms of effectiveness are cars, then banks, then travel, then alcoholic beverages of all kinds, and finally retail stores.

5. Radio listenership rates are almost unaffected by season.

6. Radio is faster than all other advertising media. So if you need to get a message out fast, radio might be best.

7. Find out how well other advertisers in your area did with radio ads before you go ahead with your own radio ads.

8. In radio, repetition gets the job done. The more often your ad airs, the better chance of hooking the mind of the listener. Also the best radio ads have a lot of 'hits.' A hit is each time your product name is mentioned. The more hits, the more effective your ad will be.

9. Start your commercial with a loud, attention getting sound to snap the listener to attention.

10. Never rely on radio alone. Radio makes up only 10% of all advertising money spent, and for good reason by itself, it won't get the job done for you. Most often, radio is an advertising medium which complements your total advertising effort. It reinforces or even directs attention to your newspaper ads.

11. Alternate the air time of your ad. If you run your ad at different times on different days, you will be sure to reach a wider number of listeners, and it will make it sound like you are running your ad more often than it actually does.

THE GREATEST STRENGTH OF RADIO IS THE FACT THAT IT EMPLOYS THE 'THEATRE OF THE MIND.'

Brainstorm 33

Newspaper ads

Advertising in newspapers is challenging, but can bring excellent results if done right. An attention-getting headline in a newspaper ad is the most important element of the ad. Your ad will compete with all the story headlines, and all the other ad headlines. That means your headline must be extra good at stopping the reader's eyes and getting them to look more deeply into your ad.

The larger the newspaper ad, the more attention and sales it will produce, but it will also cost a lot more.

Make sure your ad appears in the proper section of the newspaper. If you're selling health food, get your ad in the paper's health news page. If you sell running shoes, get it in the sports pages.

Using coupons in a newspaper ad is a great idea. It will boost response by a whole lot. Customers can clip and save your ad, and bring it in for a discount.

Running your ad just once is almost never enough. People read newspapers and then throw them away. That means your ad lasts only one day. Your ad is here and gone in a flash! The only way to overcome this is to run the ad in the same spot for a week, or two weeks, or longer.

One way to get much better results is to make your ad an advertorial. That's an ad that looks more like a regular newspaper story than an ad itself.

Make use of the classified section in newspapers to test your ads before you buy larger ads.

The best newspaper space ads have four elements:

1. Headline.
2. Body copy.
3. Photo or graphic element.
4. Your identifying signature at the bottom.

Some ads also use a subhead beneath the main headline. This helps draw the reader further into your ad.

 Brainstorm 34

TV advertising

TV advertising is a powerful, hypnotic tool that can really do wonderful things for your selling effort. Flickering lights have mesmerized human beings for centuries. TV is our modern day camp fire we sit around to tell stories – except now it's the fire itself that tells the stories, and does so with moving pictures and sound! TV advertising still comes with a 'Wow!' factor. 'As seen on TV' still means something. Yes, TV is powerful, but not without its pitfalls and problems.

Here are my Top 10 Tips for TV Advertising Excellence

1. **Use TV's main advantage – moving pictures.** The best TV ad should convey their persuasive message visually. The ultimate test of a good TV ad is being able to turn down the sound, and still get the message from the images alone.

2. **Show your product and forget the nonsense.** Many times we see commercials on TV that seem completely insane, or beside the point. Too often TV ads try to entertain at the expense of selling. Rather, use TV to show the product, create interest and desire for that product, and induce people to take action.

3. **Showing is better than telling.** Television is designed to show how a product works, not merely to tell how it works. It's far better to stage a demonstration for the viewing audience than having a handsome man or beautiful woman tell you what the product will do for you. Show what the product will get for the viewer.

4. **Use satisfied customers to sell for you.** Getting average, ordinary people on the screen to say nice things about your business is a powerful method of persuasion. It's best not to script such endorsements or testimonials. Just let people speak from their hearts about how they feel about your product. You can edit out all the stuttering and dead space later, and 'sound bite' the best lines they come up with.

5. **Avoid comparative advertising.** Comparative advertising is when you mention your competition by name, and say you are better. But when you do that, you give the competition a free plug, and it can also make you look mean. Keep the focus on your own product, and don't give any free name recognition to your competitor.

6. **Early name mention.** Identify your product quickly and repeat the identification as many times as you can. Hammer away with the repetition and you'll chip away the consumer's resistance to buy.

7. **Use emotion.** The best TV commercials appeal to emotion. A commercial showing the glowing reaction (tears of joy etc.) of a woman receiving a diamond from her husband is an excellent way to show how the product (the diamond) will create a benefit (happiness and a solidified relationship).

8. **Get attention quickly.** A TV commercial is no different from a radio or print ad in that it must get attention first. Always remember AIDA: Attention, Interest, Desire, Action. A viewer will decide in the first five seconds whether or not to pay attention to your commercial. Scream out a promise right up top – a promise to solve a problem, create a benefit, deliver something new and exciting.

9. **Show the viewer something new.** More than books or newspapers, more than magazines or radio news programs, it is TV advertising that delivers the latest information to consumers. What kind of jeans are in fashion? What is the latest hairstyle? What is the best motor oil? What new kinds of foods are available? Where are all the best restaurants located? People get this kind of information from advertising and mostly TV advertising.

10. **Target market.** Be sure your ad appears during the programs your target client is likely to watch. Men watch sports, action movies, news and more. Kids watch cartoons. Older women watch soap operas, and so on. Get viewer stats from the station manager to make sure your advertisement runs during the demographic profile that matches your product with the audience.

Brainstorm 35

Affinity sales

What business has an affinity for yours? For example, a car mechanic has an affinity with a car seller. A restaurant has an affinity with a movie theatre. A music shop has an affinity with an electronics store. All of these businesses can get together and help sell each other's customers. For example, lots of people go out for dinner and a movie. A restaurant can offer free or discount tickets to a movie with a meal, or vice versa. This way the cinema and the restaurant can send more customers to each other.

Affinity selling is another twist on joint venture or fusion marketing. You find where your interests intersect with another complementary business, and develop ways that you can help each other get more business. Don't limit your search to a partner with just one other business – look for an affinity relationship with a dozen or more businesses and you can create an avalanche of new business for yourself, and your partners.

 Brainstorm 36

Sponsored events

Even a small business can get involved in sponsoring a major event. If you're not big enough to be the exclusive sponsor, become one of several businesses sponsoring a single event.

Sponsoring can cost you next to nothing but time, services provided, or items donated. At the same time, you'll get great publicity and build your image as a company that cares.

Many events buy ads, and they list all businesses who help sponsor the event. Your name can also appear in the program in big print. Sponsoring is also an excellent networking opportunity.

Sponsoring is a fantastic way to bring in more customers while you bolster the company image as a good citizen that cares about the community. You accomplish a lot all at once.

 Brainstorm 37

Store window displays

Your store window is like a billboard that can scream out a message to the street, so don't waste this space with a mere display of your products. Use your window to give customers a reason to stop and come in. That means putting up bright, easy-to-see signs that grab attention, and then saying something specific. Use the element of 'free.' Put up a window signs that says: 'Free Ear Piercing Here!' Or, 'Get a Dinner for Two for a Test Drive!' 'Kids Eat Free!'

Also, make use of attention getting flashing lights – or maybe put a live person in your window to wink at people as they walk buy. Whatever you do, make your window on the world pull its weight by doing something exciting and different to make people stop, look, and come in.

Brainstorm 38

Special reports

Offering a free report is a powerful way to get people to respond to your ads, especially if you make the report subject matter highly interesting and with obvious value. For example, an insurance seller might state in an ad: 'Free Report: How to Get Your Insurance Provider to Pay a Claim They Have Already Rejected.' Or, an accountant can use: 'How to Save £1,500 on Taxes, Guaranteed!.' Or, a car dealer might try: 'Ten Ways to Tell if a Used Car is Junk!'

The report should deliver on its title. It can be as short as a page or two, or 20 pages long, or more. The key is getting people to ask for it, then send it to them along with your high-powered sales pitch. You should also plug yourself throughout the report, though don't make it a blatant sales plug. You offered a free report, so give them one. Do your selling later.

You may also be able to get your report advertised for free if you issue a press release saying you are giving away valuable free consumer information to the public.

Free reports can build your customer sales list fast. Every person that orders your report is another name you can mine well into the future for sales and profits.

Don't forget to offer your report in multiple formats: as an audio tape, on your web page, or even on a video.

Brainstorm 39

Press releases

The press release is a gateway to loads of free publicity. Whenever a news outlet uses your release, you get free advertising that can be hundreds of times more effective than paid advertising.

The key to getting press releases accepted and used by the media is to cater to their needs – they're looking for newsworthy information. If you provide it, newspapers, and radio and TV stations will use it.

So write your press release in news style. Put the most important information up top, and the lesser information in descending order down throughout the story. Use a provocative headline. Write in newspaper style for newspapers, in radio style for radio. There's a big difference, so study print writing style and broadcast writing style carefully before you submit. Remember that TV needs images. Thus, if you can send some video footage with your release, you stand a better chance of getting it used on TV. More likely, however, your goal will be to get a TV camera crew to come to you.

Issue a lot of press releases. Most of them will be rejected, but the more you submit, the more likely you'll score a hit.

Never forget that writing a press release is a highly refined art. Do your homework before you attempt your own. Find examples of other press releases that have worked well. Make sure you submit your release to a specific person at the media you choose – find the editor who handles the news niche you want.

Don't forget to follow-up on your release issue with a phone call. Ask the editor or reporter what you can do to make your news item more interesting, and ask what their particular needs are at the time. Help a reporter do his or her job, and you'll have a much better chance of getting your release used.

 Brainstorm 40

Magazine ads

When you want to reach a national audience, you're ready for magazine ads. You'll soon find out they're expensive. Even a short, 15-word classified ad in a major magazine can cost £200 or more. A full-page display ad in a major magazine can cost an unbelievable £100,000 and easily more! There are many small, regional magazines, however, that cost less. Small magazines also deliver a much more tightly focused market.

The most important thing to do with magazine advertising is to match your product with the right audience. This is where magazine advertising excels. Because most magazines cover a specific topic, you can be sure the readers are interested in that topic. Thus, if you sell boats, you naturally choose a nautical magazine to place your ad.

Subject-product match is more important than circulation. Many people are tempted to find the biggest circulation, and place their ads, thinking that with 10 million readers, they're bound to get good response. It rarely works that way if your product is not a good match for the magazine's audience.

Magazine ads should also be run multiple times, giving your ad a chance to find its market. A single-run ad is not a good test, unless you get terrific results right away. Then you all you have to do is keep running the ad until it stops working.

Creating your ad in the right way is also key. That means an attention grabbing headline, compelling body copy, a great offer, clear description of solid benefits, and more.

Don't forget classified ads in magazines. They tend to work much better than classified ads in newspapers. That's because they stick around longer – magazines have a longer shelf life than newspapers. They also enjoy the benefit of a highly focused target market. Use classified ads to test your magazine for response, and before you risk a high-priced display ad.

 Brainstorm 41

Consultations

One of the best ways to lure new clients is to offer a free consultation. This works especially well for professionals, such as lawyers, accountants, chiropractors, and others. It also works well for skilled service providers, such as beauty shops, clothing stores and mechanics.

You can make your free consultation offer stronger by putting a price on it, then offering it free, to wit: 'Come in for a £150 consultation free, Tuesday only!' A time limit, as the previous example shows, can make the offer even more irresistible because it creates a sense of urgency for the client to act quickly.

A consultation is an opportunity for you to access a client's needs and problems, then offers your services to meet those needs or solve those problems.

Brainstorm 42

Teleconferences

A teleconference is an exciting way to reach a captive audience, and also make each participant feel they are part of something exclusive. Many professional speakers arrange teleconferences, charging huge fees for each participant. At the same time, they can tell listeners about their product and make sales.

The most difficult aspect of the teleconference is getting people to participate. You need to advertise or use direct mail extensively to sign up enough participants to make a teleconference worthwhile. Making the event free is the best way to get a lot of participants, but if you are offering information with a high perceived value, you can also charge for the event. Whatever you do, you have to entice and convince people they are going to learn something important which will have value to their daily lives.

Teleconferences are a great way to work one-on-one with groups of people without having to travel anywhere. You can field calls from individual listeners, as well as interact with the entire listening group.

The strongest selling point of a teleconference is the aura of exclusivity. Tell people they have been selected to participate in this limited, exclusive teleconference. Remind them it's almost like attending a £1,000 seminar from the comfort of their own home – they save time and travel expenses, but at the same time, they get the full benefit of a live meeting with a real pro.

Brainstorm 43

Co-op advertising

Co-op advertising is yet another joint venture kind of activity that helps each participant reach more customers at less expense. If you are a supplier, offering to pay for 15%-50% of your retail outlet's advertising means they sell more product and buy more from you. You also get to advertise your products for 15-50% less! You can pay in either cash or merchandise. If you are a retailer, make sure you ask your supplier for a co-op advertising deal. Many retailers never ask their supplier to help pay for ads, even when the offer is standard and available from the supplier!

Another way to co-op advertise is to get together with several other businesses and buy a full page ad. Each participant gets a portion of the page, and all share in the cost of an ad.

Yet another way to co-op ad is to get another advertiser to place a plug for you directly on his ad. This works best when each player has something in common. A car dealer can work with a tyre shop. A beauty shop can advertise someone's hair care products within their ads. A pet shop can include information on dog food for a grocery store.

Use your imagination, and you can come up with many ways to cut your advertising costs by teaming up with another business in a win-win situation.

Brainstorm 44

Testimonials

None of your marketing techniques are complete, or as strong as they could be, without including testimonials. A statement by a satisfied customer is a nearly irresistible incentive for a new customer to buy. A testimonial is powerful because it represents an objective third-party endorsement of your product. When a prospect confronts a testimonial he or she is not getting just another claim by the advertiser, but a solid recommendation from an 'ordinary' guy like the prospect. A testimonial is a peer endorsement. The prospect thinks: 'This product obviously worked well for this other person, so it will probably work for me too.'

It's important to use testimonials correctly if you want them to have maximum effectiveness. We all see many ads with testimonials signed, 'Robert K., Newcastle.' This is poor use of testimonials. As only the first name is given, the prospect has reason to suspect the seller is simply making up a testimonial and attributing it to a bogus name. It's far better to get a real testimonial signed by a person with their full names, and maybe even an e-mail or phone number included with the statement. Then you have an air tight, bona fide testimonial the prospect can verify if they want to.

Testimonials are easy to obtain. Simply ask for one from a customer. Make sure you get permission to use the person's name in your advertisement and other marketing vehicles. If you're lucky, you'll get spontaneous testimonials as well. Testimonials can be a short, one-sentence statement, to a full-length feature article which tells the story of how your product made your customer's life better. Long or short, including testimonials is an absolute must!

Brainstorm 45

Celebrity endorsements

A celebrity endorsement is a superb marketing tool because it helps you gain instant access to the mind of consumers. Today the media is saturated with marketing messages from all conceivable sources. When you add your bit of clutter to all the rest, the biggest challenge is getting attention and having your marketing message seen and heard. The average prospect's mind is already 'full.' But when a celebrity endorses your product, the instant recognition they command cuts through the clutter. A celebrity helps you get into the forefront of the buyer's mind, and a celebrity's fame and notoriety rubs off on your product. Many people will stand outside in the cold rain for hours just to get a glimpse of a favourite celebrity. That's the kind of motivation you want to tap into!

But how do you get a busy, difficult-to-contact celebrity to help you out? The most obvious way is to pay the celebrity well to endorse your product. The drawback, of course, is expense. A plug from a major celebrity can mean tens of thousands, or hundreds of thousands of pounds.

But a new celebrity may help you for free so they can get some of their own exposure. Celebrities need all the free ink they can get, too! There are many other kinds of celebrities who are not major stars, but big fish in their own ponds. Examples of these might be a local DJ, a TV weatherman on your local TV station, or a local sports star. These 'minor' celebrities can work well in your own geographic marketing area, and better yet, they will be either free or affordable.

How do you contact a major celebrity? Here's what you need to do:

- Contact publicity agencies and ask which celebrities they can connect you with.

- Contact a specific celebrity's agent or publicity firm.

- Call TV stations and radio stations.

- Contact the ad agencies that have created commercials for celebrities.

- Call a celebrity's record label, publisher, studio, or athletic team.

One more idea: if you can't afford a celebrity, you might be able to get another organization to sponsor one, and then work with them to gain access for your marketing needs.

 Brainstorm 46

Customer mailing lists

Your customer mailing list is a commodity of extreme value. It is no less than the very lifeblood of your business. That's because your captured market – customers you have already sold to is your richest, easiest source of future sales.

To each person named on your list, you are a known quantity. That means no cold selling. Also, if you have provided a high quality product and excellent customer service, those people will want to continue doing business with you.

Your customer list must go beyond mere names, addresses and telephone numbers. In fact, the more detailed information you have about each name, the more powerful the customer list becomes. Here are some 'must have' customer information items:

- Type of dwelling: house, apartment, rented house?

- Size of house; number of rooms?

- Special amenities of dwelling: pool, two-door garage, solarium, exercise room?

- Special interests and/or hobbies?

- How many cars, and what kind of cars?

- Pets? How many? What kind?

- Favourite kind of movie or TV shows preferred?

- What do they read and subscribe to? Newspaper, magazine: what kind of magazines? What kind of books do they like? Romance, classic literature, horror?

- Where do they go on holiday?

- Birthdays and anniversaries?

- Town or country?

These kinds of details allow you to make your marketing messages highly specific. Why is knowing a birthday helpful, for example? If you send a birthday card to a customer who never expected one from you, they'll be flattered and delighted. If you also include a small gift and a coupon that they can use to buy a present for themselves, the customer is going to feel very special indeed. People that own houses tend to have more disposable income than renters, so you can sell higher ticket items to them.

A FREEPHONE NUMBER MAKES YOU LOOK LIKE A TOP-FLIGHT BUSINESS

Working your customer list over and over again means you make more sales than you ever thought possible. You should be mailing something to them at least a dozen times a year.

A customer list is built up over time. Every time you make a new sale, you add a name. You can use direct mail to get more names. You can hold a prize drawing which prompts people to fill in all their information for your list database.

You can even make money by renting your customer list to other sellers. In fact, renting your list for one-time-use only can bring in a very healthy amount of money. You can easily get £85 to £100 per thousand names. It's not an exaggeration to say that you can rent your list hundreds of times per year – and at a £100 per thousand names – you're looking at an excellent supplemental income stream!

 Brainstorm 47

800 numbers

Providing a freephone number for customers to call removes one more block to any potential sale. If prospects know the phone call is free, they will have much more incentive to call and buy. When you make it easy to buy, people buy more often. A freephone number makes you look like a top-flight business. A freephone number matches no specific geographic location, meaning customers from anywhere can think of you as 'local.' Getting people to call your freephone number is also an excellent way to capture names for your list-building efforts. Just advertise a 'free report' which people can hear over the phone. When they call in, an automated answering machine delivers the report or sales pitch, and also prompts people to leave their name and contact information.

You can configure your number to make it match a catchy name, such as 0-800-flowers for a flower shop. It's an attention grabber. It also describes your offer and thus helps sell it. You can make heavy use of a freephone number by putting it everywhere – on your business cards, on all your ads, in your sales letters, brochures, on TV, over the radio and on your web page.

 Brainstorm 48

Petrol pump ads

A petrol pump ad is a good way to force an advertising message on a prospect. As they wait for their car to fill with petrol, they can't help but see and maybe even stare at an ad you have strategically placed somewhere on or near the pump handle. This is another excellent place to put your freephone number. Hundreds of people will see the ad everyday, and it will be a target sampling from a wide cross section of life. You can also place a small box or poster with a pouch to provide a receptacle for your flyers or 'take-ones'.

Brainstorm 49

Yellow Pages

I firmly believe no business should be without a *Yellow Pages* ad. The best thing about the *Yellow Pages* is that people go to it when they are already ready to buy. They've decided to buy – now they're looking for a seller. *Yellow Pages* ads should be large, exciting and easy to spot. They should be more than your business name and phone number. They should have an attention grabbing headline, list your benefits, include testimonials, offer something free, and much more. The best *Yellow Pages* ads are BIG! As all your competitors will be listed along with you, often on the same page, you must do something to clearly stand out and be the first to catch the eye of the reader. A powerful headline in a large ad is a good way to get the job done.

Brainstorm 50

Balloons and other flying ads

What if your No. 1 competitor was having a big sale – and on that day you hire a balloon to float above the store flashing your name, number and a great offer! Well, one man's dirty trick is another man's aggressive competition!

What about airborne advertising messages on small airships, spotlights (smaller flying objects such as helium balloons), airplane trailers or even sky writing? Do they work? Yes they work, in a shotgun sort of way. For example, let's say a man is driving down a busy street thinking about what he should get his young son for a birthday present. He looks up and suddenly sees a huge hot air balloon that has a gigantic picture of a Spider Man on it, and the name of a hobby shop beneath it. His gift idea is solved and he drives over to the hobby shop to buy a Spider-Man piece of merchandise.

Big ads in the sky do one very important thing in advertising very well – they get large numbers of people to stop and notice. If done right, you can even target market with sky advertising. For example, an airplane pulling a sign by a crowded beach can advertise surf boards, boats or bathing suits. Right market, right message – it gets noticed and gets results.

 Brainstorm 51

Word-of-mouth

Word-of-mouth advertising is among the very best kinds of advertising, and one of the most important techniques any business must learn to master. When one person tells another person about your business and recommends it, that's an almost guaranteed sale ready to happen.

Sometimes word-of-mouth, or WOM, happens spontaneously. When a company provides an exciting new product that a lot of people need, and then back it up with superior customer service, it creates an unstoppable buzz that translates into robust sales – and best of all, the company pays for none of it because the people are out there spreading your message for free.

We've already revealed one of the keys to creating WOM: exciting products that solve problems or fulfil needs, backed-up by caring, attentive customer service. Do that, and you'll get your WOM going.

But you can also be proactive in starting WOM. You can pay or 'bribe' people to tell other people about you. One way is to get compelling, positive stories about yourself in the media. If a few thousand people see how your product helped someone on the local TV news, or in the local paper, they'll talk about it with their friends, and spread your message.

 Brainstorm 52

T-shirt ads

How do you get hundreds of people to be walking billboards advertising your company or product? Easy – give them a free T-shirt with all the relevant information on it. Many people will even pay to wear your T-shirt if they like the design enough. You sell them at £10 each, and get your ad carried along for nothing! You can combine a T-shirt ad campaign with the concept of getting something free if you offer a complementary T-shirt with the purchase of a specific amount or a particular product. Or, you can use them to get people to come to a special sale; 'Come in and get a free T-shirt today!' Make sure you design a T-shirt that works to sell. That means more than just your name or logo – try to get some activation information, like a freephone number included. If you're clever enough, you can design your T-shirt to be both attractive to wear, and have enough utility to get the work of promotion done.

Brainstorm 53

Statement stuffers

Make your customer billing statements do some extra work by making them carry along a marketing message. It's almost like free advertising because you're doing the mailing anyway, and the customer is most likely paying for shipping. The best ideas for statement stuffers are:

- Tell the customer something they don't know about your business.

- A contest entry form guaranteed to get customers to respond which also gives you more information about the customers.

- Announce an upcoming sale.

- An ad for a back-end product, or an up-sell message.

- Ask your customer to attend a charity event you are sponsoring.

- Announce or introduce a new product.

You can also get other companies to agree to stuff your message into their billing statements. It's far easier than you think. If the company likes your idea, if your stuffer delivers value to the customer, many agree without a hitch. If you attach a charity element to the stuffer, it will be even easier to get your stuffer to ride along free to thousands of customers who belong to another company. Just combine your charity message with your selling information, and you have it made!

Brainstorm 54

Seminars

Giving your own seminar, or agreeing to appear at someone else's seminar, is one of the best marketing strategies I can think of. If you move into a new town where you are unknown, presenting a series of seminars can take you from an unknown to a widely well-known in just weeks.

Speaking at seminars positions you as an expert in your field. Every person who attends your seminar is another name for your customer list. You can make a large amount of sales right on the spot when you give a seminar. A seminar is an excellent way to attract free publicity. Invite reporters and then give exciting, useful and newsworthy information in your seminar, and the free ink will be rolling out as fast as the presses can print!

You can even get paid to promote yourself if you charge a fee to attend your seminar. In this case, you better have something very valuable at your seminar to prompt people to pay. For example, I have a friend who moved to Seattle where she knew no one, and no one knew her. Her business was massage therapy. She put on a series of seminars entitled: *'How to beat migraine headache pain without drugs.'* Another was: *'How to rid yourself of back pain without medicine.'*

The response was heavy. Thousands of people suffer head and back pain, and they're looking for solutions that don't involve expensive and mind-numbing pain killing drugs. At the seminar, she touted massage therapy as an alternative, and she provided strong 'prove it' information to convince people that massage was an excellent solution. Before long, and without buying a single ad, she was flooded with business, and soon hired two more massage staff to meet the demand!

Want things to start happening for your business? Then give seminars – and you'll have more business than you can possible handle – fast!

 Brainstorm 55

Voice mail

Setting up a voice mail number people can call to hear your sales pitch is a non-labour intensive way to reach thousands of people fast and inexpensively. Write a two minute sales pitch people can call free and listen to. Then advertise your number aggressively, and wait for the calls to pour in. Your voice mail does the selling for you, can take orders, and complete the entire sales process. You can sell to thousands of people while you spend your time doing something else. The key is to have a compelling script that sells well. Your voice mail can also be used for advertising, and prompt the caller to come in, or order your more complete marketing package. Voice mail is a technology that sells, and also frees you to spend time on other forms of selling – but if it works really well, you could spend your time on the beach while your voice mail generates the cash!

GIVE SEMINARS – AND YOU'LL HAVE MORE BUSINESS THAN YOU CAN POSSIBLE HANDLE – FAST!

Brainstorm 56

Fax marketing, fax selling

With a fax machine, you can simultaneously broadcast your marketing message to thousands of people with the speed of a single telephone call. That means you can reach enormous amounts of people in just a blink. You don't have to wait for the post office to deliver your marketing messages, and wait even longer for response. Thus, faxing your marketing messages gets your cash flow jump started fast.

Fax broadcasting also costs less than direct mail because there's no postage, no printing costs and other mailing costs, such as need for envelopes, stuffing envelopes, and so on.

Fax broadcasting has several drawbacks. The irritation factor is high because many people do not appreciate having their own fax paper being used for your marketing message. Fax broadcasting is also prohibited in many locations. The term 'junk fax' is gaining steam and junk faxes are reviled more than regular junk mail by many.

On the other hand, a fax is hard to ignore. People must confront it, take it from the machine and look at it – that's 75% of the battle!

Brainstorm 57

Fax-on-demand

Perhaps a better way to use the fax in marketing is fax on demand. In this scenario, people call your advertised number and an automated system faxes your sales material right back to them. It's also more economical than direct mail. It reaches everywhere – even around the world with ease.

Fax-on-demand can be an ideal solution for those who are swamped with telephone calls from people needing more information about their product. It can also be an excellent alternative to reach people who don't have Internet access, and can't get the same info from your web page.

If you advertise your fax-on-demand number aggressively, it can effortlessly distribute your marketing messages to thousands of people per day, costing you no more than the phone charges.

Your fax must have all the hallmarks of excellent sales letters – attention grabbing headlines, compelling sales copy, benefits described, order form, a terrific offer and all the rest. Don't forget that all callers are one more bit of information captured for your customer database. You get their fax number for future use.

Brainstorm 58

Referrals

Ask any experienced seller and they'll tell you: "90% of my business comes from referrals." It's a fact that more business probably comes from referrals than any other source – more than your advertising, more than direct mail, more than telecanvassing – it's that important.

You get referrals from three sources: 1. Current customers 2. Inactive customers, and 3. Anyone who has contact with your customer or potential customers.

These six conditions are necessary for the above three to generate referrals:

1. The referral agent must have frequent contact with your customers.

2. The referral agent must be trusted and respected by customers.

3. The referral agent must be actively prompted to make referrals.

4. The referral agent should be able to weed out poorly qualified customers.

5. The referral agent must like you, and trust you.

6. The referral agent must have some motivation to do what you want – make referrals!

So the key for you is to identify prime referral agent candidates and then meet with them. Give them a reason to refer customers to you. It might take a cut of the business, like a small commission on each sale, or something less tangible. There are many ways for one person to scratch your back if you scratch theirs. An agreement between two non-competing business to send customers to each other is a superb idea.

Brainstorm 59

Radio/TV interviews

An excellent way to get free publicity is to make yourself available for interviews by radio and TV reporters. The key is getting invited. How do you do that?

First, make sure you are listed in professional directories. When reporters need an expert to come in, they often look in *Who's Who* or other directories to find an expert.

Second, if you position yourself as an expert, you'll be on the media shortlist for an interview. If you write a book in your field and send it to all media people, you'll be considered a good interview on the subject you have written about. Giving frequent seminars and publishing a newsletter is another way to position yourself in your community as an expert. Make sure all reporters are on your newsletter mailing list, and that they get invited to your seminar.

Another key to getting on radio or TV is to know what their content needs are, and provide it. For example, many radio and TV news programs have health segments, which provide healthy living information to the audience. This is a golden opportunity for dentists, health food stores owners, chiropractors, doctors and more to get invited for an interview about the latest health topic. Send a press release to the editor of the health news segment and suggest a topic, and offer yourself as an interviewee. This method works extremely well, and is not limited to any one field. A businessman, an auto mechanic, a pet store owner, a hair stylist – all can provide newsworthy info in their respective fields that would make good radio and TV feature material.

 Brainstorm 60

TV infomercials

Producing your own 30-minute TV infomercial can be a fast way to untold millions in sales – or to disaster! When infomercials first burst on the scene, a few dozen people became millionaires overnight! The newness of the medium and format of the infomercial was enough to sell just about anything. But when hundreds of others wanted a piece of the easy money pie, the airwaves got crowded with dozens of infomercials, making them the bane of TV viewers everywhere. That meant a lot of failed infomercials, and lots of money lost. Yet, many infomercials still work, and work spectacularly well.

TV infomercials are very expensive, and work best when a celebrity helps sell the product. To run your infomercial, you need to buy large blocks of TV time, which is also very expensive.

The best infomercial products:

- Have mass appeal.
- Are unique.
- Are high quality.

- Have the perception of a fantastic price for the product.
- Make for entertaining demonstration.
- Have the ability to generate good conversation by hosts.
- Are faddish, trendy, cutting edge.

To get into infomercial marketing, you need to seek out seasoned pros to help you make your video, to negotiate airtime with TV stations, hire professional actors, if not celebrities, and you need to be prepared with a large inventory of products to ship immediately. Look in the *Yellow Pages* for an agent that handles infomercial business.

Infomercials are high risk, high excitement, high powered marketing vehicles that are not for the faint of heart. They tend to be boom or bust undertakings, making either truck loads of money, or costing the advertiser a truck load of lost cash. Study the industry carefully and get advice from experienced pros before you jump into the infomercial world – but never rule it out for yourself. Just approach it with care and intelligence, and move forward only when you have tested your product in other ways to make sure you know demand for your product is high enough to make it infomercial material.

... AN INFOMERCIAL CAN BE A FAST WAY TO UNTOLD MILLIONS IN SALES – OR TO DISASTER!

Brainstorm 61

Flyers/handouts

Using flyers is a great way to 'deep prospect' a particular geographic area. Flyers have many advantages over letters sent through the mail. First, you pay no postage. Second, you don't have to work hard to get potential customers to open them – they're 'in the face' of the prospect upon delivery. They're cheaper to print, and they take less time to read than full-length sales letters.

Distributing flyers can be done by children or teenagers – or anyone looking to make a few extra dollars on a long afternoon. Even non-profit groups, such as the Boy Scouts or ball clubs looking to raise money to support their team can be enlisted to be your personal 'flyer distribution army.' Just put up an ad in a coin operated laundry, the free ads magazine or local circular and you'll find a lot of takers to handle the foot work.

If you distribute your flyers in an area that has a need for what you're selling, response rates can easily be as high as 15%. When you consider direct mailers are ecstatic with 2% response, flyers look very attractive indeed.

Flyers should be tested to determine how well they work. Fortunately, that's easy to do. Simply code your flyers by colour, with numbers, or with letters of the alphabet, and then see which ones bring back the best results.

Flyers will only work as well as the offer you make on them. Use all the techniques I've been touting throughout this book: sizzling sales copy, a free offer, benefits, a catchy headline, and easy contact info … and all the rest!

Brainstorm 62

Fundraisers

Helping out with a fund raiser for a good cause will help out your marketing cause as well. Again, when you do good works, you bolster your image as a company who cares, and you create opportunities for free media coverage. Get hooked up with a charity that best matches your customer demographic. Ask what you can do to help. Every fundraising contact you make should also contain a plug for your business – just be sure you don't make yourself look like you're more concerned with the marketing than the fundraising.

A great way to raise funds for charity and sell your products simultaneously is to donate a set amount for each purchase made. For example, you might say: "One pound of every purchase will be donated to the Feed the Children Fund." You tie selling to a good cause, and everybody wins!

 Brainstorm 63

Gifts

It is better to give than to receive. We all know that! And in business, you also get a lot when you give even just a little. The 'free gift' is one of the most used and popular marketing tools – and why not? It almost never fails to work. We're talking about the concept of 'free,' one of the single most powerful motivators known in marketing. There are many ways you can work the free gift concept into your strategy. 'Free gift when you purchase X!' After a purchase is made, why not surprise a customer with a free gift they never expected to get? This is a particularly powerful tactic. When a customer gets more than they expected to get, the impact is deep and lasting. You create repeat business and strong customer loyalty. Many marketers quake at the idea of giving free gifts because of the expense. But that's short-sighted. When you give, you are going to get back much more. You don't have to give away the farm to offer something free. As in ordinary gift giving, we all know 'it's the thought that counts.' This is definitely true in business as well. When you make the gesture, you create the positive perception that your company is a generous, caring company that has more than the bottom line in mind. Incidentally, the term 'free gift' drives some people crazy because if a gift isn't free, how can it be a gift? Imagine a 'gift' that you have to pay for!! Still, adding the word 'free' to gift simply makes the offer look stronger, so it's a redundancy we live with – and to heck with the grammar snobs!

 Brainstorm 64

Gift vouchers

I mentioned this earlier but it's worth saying again! A gift voucher is a great way to 'sell paper.' When you sell a gift voucher, the buyer pays now and gets the product later. That's a strong cash flow advantage for you. Just about every business uses gift vouchers, but few of them use them as creatively as they might. Most companies are too passive in offering gift vouchers. Rather than simply letting customers know you have gift vouchers available, I suggest an aggressive, proactive approach to get prospects to buy more gift vouchers faster. One way to do that is to design a direct mail piece dedicated to pushing gift vouchers. Send your mailer two months before Christmas, for example, and tell prospects they can get their shopping done early and effortlessly by purchasing a gift voucher now.

Or why not let customers know that your gift vouchers will get them a 15% discount over a regular purchase. The customer gets more buying clout for the buck with a voucher. It will motivate them to buy. Another idea is to bribe the customer into buying a gift voucher. That means a free gift voucher with the purchase of a gift voucher. For example, for every £50 gift voucher bought, the buyer gets a £5 discount voucher they can use towards a future purchase.

Use gift vouchers, but put some life into the practice by coming up with ways to sell a lot of them fast. Offer special incentives, push the idea of convenience, tell customers their loved ones will love them more if they give them one of your gift vouchers. Gift vouchers are a good marketing tool that should be modified for maximum potential. Don't forget gift vouchers are an excellent way to raise 'fast cash' (see Section 6).

 Brainstorm 65

Newsletter inserts

Contributing to other people's newsletters with articles or inserts is an inexpensive and excellent way to reach new markets and tap into the captured customers of another business. Most newsletter publishers welcome submissions from others because finding content for newsletters is an ongoing challenge. If you provide them with non-competing information, you can easily gain access to another company's newsletter. For example, a massage therapist might submit to a chiropractor's newsletter. The services are similar enough to appeal to the same audience, but different enough to offer distinct services. You can either submit a story, or provide an insert to the newsletter publisher. In the latter case, it works much like a joint mailing. You help defray the cost of mailing the newsletter in exchange for letting your insert ride along. Both parties win.

Newsletter inserts have the strong advantage of delivering highly focused markets. When you insert in a regular newspaper, you're getting a general audience. But if you're in the car valeting business, for example, getting your insert into a car seller's newsletter hits the car buyer/owner/enthusiast directly. I can't say enough about the power of highly focused, very tight target marketing. You zero in on highly qualified customers, and waste no resources on shotgun approaches made to a general audience. Newsletter inserts are likely to be far cheaper than general publications, and you can even arrange a barter – get your insert free if you accept an insert from your host in your newsletter.

 Brainstorm 66

Magazine inserts

Most magazine inserts take the form of a card stapled or placed loose into the binding of the magazine. They have the advantage of irritating the reader. Why is that an advantage? Because it forces the reader to confront the card, and deal with it – most often throw it out. But before they do that, they'll almost always look at it, and if they like what they see, they'll take action on it.

The magazine insert is vastly underused by most sellers today. When you say insert, most marketers automatically think 'newspaper.' That's where you use inserts, right? Well, yes, but why not magazines? They have the tremendous advantage of being highly audience specific, while newspapers are for general audiences. If you're selling high-tech wood burning stoves, finding a home improvement magazine will deliver the perfect audience. Perhaps the biggest drawback of magazine inserts is expense. High profile magazines with national audiences don't come cheap, and many will reject your insert anyway. But look for smaller, regional magazines. These are a golden opportunity to use as a vehicle for your inserts. You'll get a more targeted audience, both by geography and subject.

 Brainstorm 67

Newspaper inserts

Okay, let's talk about the well-known newspaper insert. As much as magazine inserts are underused, these are perhaps the most used kind of print advertising. Every day a half-dozen or more inserts come stuffed in your paper. The competition and clutter is great, meaning you have to work harder to get noticed. How many times have you opened your newspaper, only to have a stack of inserts fall out so that you can throw them directly into the bin? That's the disadvantage of the newspaper insert: there's a high rate of customer apathy. On the other hand, you can be sure that a certain percentage of newspaper readers live for inserts and coupons. They go through them carefully looking for bargains and discount coupons. These are valuable people to reach, making inserts worthwhile.

The vast majority of inserts come in the Sunday paper, so maybe you should choose a day when circulation traffic is weakest in the paper. Monday is a good day for low traffic, although circulation tends to be weak too, meaning you reach fewer people – though that's not always a bad thing when you have a more captive and focused audience.

Remember that you can get your supplier to pay for your inserts if you make the right agreement with them. Perhaps the most important thing to remember about inserts is to make yours different from the rest, and don't fall into the trap of issuing only institutional, do-nothing inserts that make all the same-old offers the rest do. Rather, produce bold, attention grabbing headlines that lead directly into strong sales copy that hammer away at benefits and which makes a strong offer. Include a discount coupon for better results, and include your freephone number. Use inserts, but think different! Think attention! Think surprise! Think about waking up the consumer!

 Brainstorm 68

In-package advertising

If you have made a sale and you're shipping a product anyway, it only makes sense to use that vehicle for more of your marketing materials to ride along with it. Insert your best direct mail materials inside the package you're shipping to a sold customer, and go for the second sale right away. Not including more sales materials in your packages is a lost opportunity to up-sell, back-end sell, and add-on sell – and it's these latter kinds of sales where real profits are really made!

Brainstorm 69

Package advertising

What's on the outside of your packages? Nothing, you say? Why? Why are you wasting a space you know your customer is going to look at? Why not print ads, your freephone number or even a coupon on the outside of the package? You can also attach a sealed envelope to the outside of the package. The customer will almost always open it. They may think it's an invoice or some other important information about the purchase they have just received. But if they open it and get something they never expected to get – like a coupon with a nice discount on a future purchase – you'll enjoy that added value effect which works so well in selling.

Brainstorm 70

Bumper stickers

Bumper stickers are a good way to advertise because:

- They're like a travelling business card.
- They reach a captive audience.
- The message is brief and easy to absorb.
- They can generate curiosity.
- They make people think.
- They can generate word of mouth.
- They easily capture attention.

Everybody likes them because they tend to be funny.

WHAT'S ON THE OUTSIDE OF YOUR PACKAGES? NOTHING? WHY?

Just remember – funny doesn't necessarily sell – benefits sells and activation information bring people to your store, or gets them to call you.

If you play your cards right (or your stickers right!) you can get thousands of people in your area to drive around with your ad on the back of their cars! For example, a quick oil change service owner told each customer they'd get a £2 discount on their oil change if they agreed to drive away with a bumper sticker on the car. The sticker read: 'Fresh oil fast! Speedy Lube, 7th and Hill Ave.' Within 60 days, more than 5,000 cars were travelling the city carrying this terrific ad seen by thousands of people each day!

Maximize your bumper sticker effort by transferring your message to T-shirts, hats, cup holders, pens, etc.

Brainstorm 71

Letters to editors

One way just about anyone can get published in any newspaper is to write a letter to the editor. To the marketer, this presents opportunity – an opportunity for some free press, that is.

The key is to work a promotional message into your letter, without making it look that way. Have no doubt, there's nothing more repulsive to an editor than someone who will try to use the hallowed editorial page as a vehicle for some kind of PR plug. Newspapers consider their editorial pages as sacred ground. No ads are run there, paid or otherwise. It's intended to be a forum for the pure exchange of ideas. Furthermore, editors are extremely discriminating readers, and they can spot a blatant PR pitch from a light year away.

Knowing all this would seem to make it impossible to use a letter to the editor as a pitch for your business. Well, maybe you can't work in a pitch, but you can get your name, and the name of your business in print in one of the most highly read sections of the newspaper.

The best idea is to respond to a story that has already run in the paper, or better yet, one of the newspaper's editorials, or a response to a letter from another reader. You can also write a letter on a topic of high interest, relevance which is on people's minds.

It's very important that you don't write an angry, controversial letter, or blast someone else for something they did or said you don't agree with. Rather, write a positive letter making constructive comments and suggestions. It's okay if you 'hit a nerve' as long as you're sure most people will agree with the way you do it!

In the text of your letter, you can find a way to identify yourself, and you may even be able to tie that into what you do for a living. For example, if you're a car dealer, you might write a letter about the need for more traffic signals in a school zone where children often cross the street. Your letter may say something like:

... The intersection at High St. and Acacia Avenue is in dire need of a new set of pedestrian lights. Hundreds of children must cross there each day on their way to school and back. There have been too many close calls lately, so I think the rate payers of this town should foot the bill for traffic lights that will make crossing safe and easy for our children. As a person who sells cars in this town, the last thing I want is someone getting hurt by a motorist that didn't have greater reason to slow down or stop with so many children around.

Sincerely,
Bob Anderson

When people read this letter, they will see that Bob Anderson sells cars! It's not an ad, it's not hard sell – but it is Bob's name in print, and it also states his business. That's one more bit of publicity that puts Bob on the path to becoming a household name in his geographic marketing arena.

If Bob made a point to write at least a dozen letters a year, the impact of getting his name on the highly read editorial page is going to be significant. Don't underestimate the value of getting your name in print as often as you can, and in a positive light. Letters to the Editor are one way of doing just that.

Brainstorm 72

Demonstrations

Did you know that the sales demonstration is a little science in itself? Demonstrating successfully is a primary key in closing a sale when you sell face-to-face. Also, conducting public demonstrations of your product is a powerful way to multiply sales fast. Maybe you've been in a shopping mall and happened upon a person demonstrating a new line of cooking wear. If the demonstrator was a talented entertainer and you were drawn in, you may have been enticed to get a set of those pots and pans, even if that's the last thing you needed at that moment! That's the power of demonstrations!

People who sell one-on-one must also master the art of demonstrating their product. Here are the keys to successful demonstrations:

- Know what to demonstrate before you get started. That means finding out what the prospect wants and needs to know so that you can show them how the product will get them what they want. You find out what they want with a needs assessment of the prospect before you start demonstrating. You perform a needs assessment by asking key questions to find out what's important to them.

- Get the prospect involved in your demonstration. Let him or her get their hands on the item so they can 'experience' the product with their own senses of touch, smell, sight, sound and even taste if it applies. When you engage the senses, you're well on your way!

- Be careful of your own physical positioning in relation to the prospect while you demonstrate. Don't violate a customer's personal body space. Rather, place yourself in an unthreatening stance above, alongside or opposite the prospect.

- A prospect has 'two brains' – emotional and rational. The emotional is the stronger of the two, so appeal to it for a more compelling demonstration.

- Get the prospect to visualise himself or herself owning the product. Make them see themselves in a better position by owning the product.

- When demonstrating to a group, seek to identify the leader in that group and align yourself with that person verbally, through eye contact, and with body language. The others in the group tend to instinctively follow the leader.

- Create a positive selling environment. That means eliminating distractions and placing yourself in a position of strength, such as being above the client. At the very least, avoid selling from a lower position relative to the prospect, which can create a perception of weakness.

- Avoid the subject of price until after you show how the product satisfies needs and emotional wants.

- Remember that people buy for two reasons:
  1. For what the product will do for them, get for them, or satisfy in them,
  2. To make themselves look good to others and especially to a spouse, significant other, close friend or neighbour.

Master these demonstration techniques, and you'll be an irresistible selling machine!

Brainstorm 73

Taxi ads

Taxi cabs are a common sight in any city of size. You see them zipping about everywhere, waiting on corners, stopping for a fare. And you sometimes see a sign on the side advertising everything from apples to zithers. But do these ads work? Do they pull response? Do they get people to call? I'm happy to say the answer is yes! Taxi cab ads do something the best outdoor advertising can do – they move around and get attention. And they go just about everywhere, so lots of different target markets see them. A cab ad may not be right for every business, but they're right for a lot of them. It's well worthwhile testing a taxi advertisement. Try your free-phone number, or get a high-impact, punchy slogan to ride around town and track your results carefully. A taxi ad can be an excellent supplement or catalyst for your other high profile advertising and promotion efforts. They can also get your phone ringing.

 Brainstorm 74

Newspaper/magazine columns

Writing and publishing a periodic column is a superb marketing strategy. First, a column, like a book, is a powerful positioning tool. When your name and thumbnail photo appears over your column week-to-week, you build your reputation as an expert in your field. When it comes time to buy, your name will be front and centre in the customer's mind. Furthermore, you'll be perceived as superior to your competitors because 'you're the guy who writes that column!' Second, every column you publish is better than any ad you can buy, especially if you cleverly work your marketing messages into your 'objective' information. A news or informational column is not perceived as an ad, and thus, turns off the buyer's natural mental 'ad filter.' Everybody knows that all ads are filled with hype – but a column? No, that's straight news, and thus, commands a high degree of credibility. The tough part is getting a newspaper or magazine to agree to run your column. Publishers absolutely hate handing out free ink to anybody, and they won't like your column if it's a blatant attempt to plug your business. So instead, write an honest-to-goodness column that provides solid information readers can use, or be entertained by. Tagging your freephone number at the end of your column may be all you need to get your phone ringing. A good, subtle writer can work in 'hidden' pitches for his or her products, but it must be done with the utmost finesse. Offer your column for free to any publisher who will run it. That way they get something and you get something. If they run your column, you have a blockbuster tool for garnering new business, and you'll solidify your image as the best at what you do!

 Brainstorm 75

Calendars

Giving away free calendars to your prospects is a legendary way to put your name, number and product in front of buyers, and keep it there for the entire year. The bottom line is that calendars work. They are perhaps the best 'premium' you can offer your customers as a free gift. Few people will refuse a gift calendar. They'll look at it just about every day, and when it's time to buy – hey presto! – your name is right there! So get yourself to a printer or calendar dealer and get yours printed up today. You'll be glad you did.

Brainstorm 76

Direct mail

Direct mail should be a primary weapon in the selling arsenal of anyone in the business of selling anything. You could be peddling £80,000,000 jet fighters, or little wooden dolls for a couple of pounds each – and direct mail will help you sell those products better! I guarantee it! Direct mail is a fantastic deal for your marketing pound. If you generate as little as 1% response, you're probably going to make money. Generate 2% and better, and you're going to have spectacular success, and truly wonderful profits! This doesn't mean that direct mail can't fail. It does all the time. It fails because naive marketers don't take the time to learn and implement direct marketing the right way. Here are the primary reasons direct marketing campaigns fail:

- Mailing pieces with substandard copy writing.

- Bad headlines on sales letters, brochures, etc.

- Bad mailing lists.

- Not including a money-back guarantee.

- Not making a terrific, 'can't refuse' offer.

- Not offering something free.

- Not using a discount coupon.

- Not having a back-end or added value follow up product.

- Not following up with second and third mailings if necessary.

- Not including testimonials.

- Forgetting a P.S. (the most read part of a sales letter!).

- Confusing order forms.

- Not putting teaser copy on outside of the envelope to get them opened.

- Not using 'prove it' copy.

- Not clearly communicating benefits.

- Heavy emphasis on features, rather than benefits.

- Failing to include a freephone number.

- Making it difficult to pay (not giving choices, such as credit card, etc).

- Failing to rigorously test results.

... and there may be one or two more, but these are certainly the biggies.

Search out and study at least a couple of dozen other successful mail pieces before you start your own. Get advice from a pro. But don't procrastinate. I urge you to develop your direct mail piece as soon as you can and get this marketing powerhouse method working for you now! Direct mail is fun, exciting, profitable, and even addictive! And that's the kind of positive addiction a seller can thrive upon!

DIRECT MAIL IS A FANTASTIC DEAL FOR YOUR MARKETING POUND.

WHEN YOU HELP OTHER PEOPLE WITH DONATIONS, GOOD THINGS HAPPEN FOR YOUR BUSINESS. BELIEVE IT!

 Brainstorm 77

Donations

Making donations to worthy causes generates publicity, and builds your image as a company with a heart. Why is that so important? Because people buy from companies they like. Whether prospects like you or not is far more important to them than who has the lowest price! It's more important than convenience. It can even be more important than quality! I assure you, the 'likeability' factor is that strong, that powerful and that important. When you help people, when you make a generous donation, or even a token donation, you enhance that all important positive image factor that makes customers choose you over a competitor. Making a donation is also an excellent reason to submit a press release which can get you free coverage in the press – and free press coverage can be 2,000% more effective than paid for advertising! If you're not convinced by now that making donations to good causes – and making sure you get credit for it – is a terrific idea, please read this paragraph again! When you help other people with donations, good things happen for your business. Believe it!

Brainstorm 78

Samples

If you're shopping for groceries, and you happen to be hungry, it's amazing how good those little free samples of hot pizza or sausages-on-a-toothpick taste, isn't it? Man, it's difficult not to pick up one of those frozen pizzas at that moment! That's a small example of why free samples are such a good marketing tool. Experienced marketers know that if they can just get a sample of their product into the hands (or the mouth!) of a prospect so they can experience it directly, a sale is not far away. That's why car dealers urge people to come in for a test drive. That's why so many sellers let you 'try it free for 30 days or pay nothing.' It's why perfume sellers pay sky-high advertising rates to put a 'scratch and sniff' sample of their heavenly scent in the pages of a magazine. They know an actual physical sample in the hands of the prospect is 100 times better than a mere picture of a product in a catalogue, or a description of a product in advertising sales copy. When the prospect can see, hear, smell, touch and taste the product, they'll literally sell themselves. Also, people love to get something for free. Free samples are an excellent way to draw people in, and get them closer to the product so they can experience it, then buy it.

PEOPLE LOVE TO GET SOMETHING FOR FREE. FREE SAMPLES ARE AN EXCELLENT WAY TO DRAW PEOPLE IN.

Brainstorm 79

Directories

According to the Association of Industrial Advertisers, about 35% of buyers looking for sellers find those sellers in business directories! Are you listed in any directories right now? If not, why not? Many of them will list you for free! Others will charge you to be listed, but it's well worth it. Right now, there are thousands of buyers out there ready to make a purchase, and they're searching through a business directory for a seller. One of those sellers should be you! Also, editors and reporters use directories to find an 'expert' for a story they are writing. If they call you, you'll get free ink. Furthermore, seminar and trade show organizers use business directories to find speakers for their events – more free promotion opportunity for you. Examples of directories are the Who's Who series that come in many categories. There are dozens of other directories as well, many of them aimed at specific industries. Don't pass over this opportunity to reach all new markets, some of which you may have never discovered otherwise!

 Brainstorm 80

Exhibits

An exhibit has a somewhat academic sound to it. You expect to find an exhibit at a science fair or technology trade show. But what an exhibit basically gets down to is a chance to show off and demonstrate your product in a public setting, and that means a chance to reach new customers. You can exhibit at trade shows, fairs, flea markets, shopping malls or even in a parking lot! Call it what you want as long as you come prepared to attract customers, get attention, add names to your customer lists, distribute sales literature, and get people to make direct contact with what you're selling. Make your exhibit fun, entertaining, inviting and hands on. The end results will be dozens or hundreds of new leads, and lots of sales right on your exhibit site.

 Brainstorm 81

Website

Anyone selling anything today should have at least some kind of presence on the World Wide Web. There is no reason not to. Even if you have next to no budget for a web page, you can get one anyway because of the variety of free web hosting services available. All it will cost you is your time to construct your page, and then administer it, and that time can be minimal because of the automated features used to run web pages. Even a free web page can be aggressively listed on search engines and reach a gigantic audience. No one can afford to pass up any opportunity to get free exposure for their business and product – the Web is just that. Let's face it – although the Web is fraught with challenges and pitfalls, it's still the way of the future. Sooner or later, the Web is going to be 'where it's at!' You can also decide to be more aggressive by pouring some time, money and resources into a web page, making it your primary, or a major marketing strategy. That means paying for your own domain space, hiring a pro to design a top-flight web page, spending money to advertise it, getting listed on top search engines, and pushing it as far as you can.

The web can be your primary mode of doing business, but it can also be a supporting role for your existing, traditional business. Even if you choose not to sell directly through your website, it can be a powerful promotion tool, research tool, and a way to find all new markets and potentially millions of new customers. A web page gives you instant global reach – anywhere the web goes, you can go to sell your products. At no other time in history has reaching a global market been so remarkably easy and inexpensive. To not recognize this potential and to not start dabbling with it, even on a limited scale, simply makes no sense. The bottom line – use the web!

 Brainstorm 82

Associate e-marketing

Combining your effort with other web entrepreneurs is a win-win strategy that can do wonders for your business. Imagine gaining access to thousands of new customers instantly! You do that by exchanging your web-based customer base with another web seller's customer base. If your businesses are complimentary, the results can be swift and profitable. Make an agreement to let a friend sell to your customers if you can sell to theirs. Use each other's captured e-mail lists to piggy-back your marketing messages on each other's. Combining efforts in this way can cost almost nothing, but generate amazing income. That's an opportunity just too rich too ignore. Start searching for a web partner today and explore the possibilities. Make sure you link up with an entity you can be proud to be associated with, and also do your best to represent your partner well. The two of you together – or three or four of you together – multiply your individual efforts accordingly. This is one of the fastest ways to bolster cash flow and find new markets.

Brainstorm 83

Billboards

Billboards are everywhere. How many did you see today when you drove to and from work? A couple of hundred? A couple of thousand? How many do you remember? And don't forget signs, banners, electronic signs, window signs, magnetic signs on cars and trucks, signs painted on the entire sides of buildings. This billboard proliferation phenomenon points to an immediate problem – how does yours compete with all the clutter?

Well, the bottom line is that signs and billboards do work, despite all the competition, but you must design your outdoor advertising right to make sure you get noticed. A roadside billboard must deliver its message in less than five seconds! Your marketing message must be seen and absorbed in a flash. Thus, your billboard must be simple and direct, and have a punchy, very short, high-impact message. Your outdoor advertising must work hard to attract attention. Those that do it best are electronic – they flash, blink, blaze – crackle, sizzle, pop! Having a sign on which you can change the lettering every day is also a great idea. Still another great idea is a sign that imitates your business, so to speak. For example, a sign shaped like a big flower for a flower shop, or a dog for a pet store. Signs that travel have been shown to work extremely well – such as signs on buses, or on taxi cabs.

So use signs and billboards, but don't be just another piece of clutter. Work hard to get your outdoor advertising noticed!

Brainstorm 84

Piggy-back mailings

One of the fastest and cheapest ways to reach thousands of new customers is the piggy-back mailing. Approach another company and make a deal to have them stuff your advertisement along with their business mailings. You get instant access to their customers, and you pay less because you both share the cost of mailing. Be creative in your choice of hosts. How about the electric company? They reach everyone, and you can be sure the mailer will be opened, which is one of the biggest challenges in direct mail! Make sure you find a non-competing, complementary business you won't mind being associated with.

 Brainstorm 85

Joint ventures

A joint venture can be as simple as exchanging e-mail lists with another company, or piggy back mailings – to developing deeper relationships with others to help you both sell more products. The basic idea is to get access to each other's customers. A car dealer gives a gift voucher for a free steak dinner at a local restaurant with the purchase of a car. An accountant writes a letter to all his clients endorsing an attorney, or vice versa. A clothing store places mannequins dressed in pyjamas in a mattress seller's shop. McDonald's sells Coke with its burgers – it's a classic joint venture. The possibilities are endless. Everywhere you go, every business you visit is a potential idea for cooperation. Chance favours the prepared mind!

Brainstorm 86

Endorsed mailings

When a known, respected person or business sends a letter to customers telling them how great you are, you'll get lots of new business fast. All you need to do is to get someone to do it for you! Endorsement letters work because it's a third-party plug which makes that plug more accepting and credible. Endorsement letters also have an added-value effect: when the return address on the letter is from a person the reader knows, but then finds a message of praise for someone they don't know, it's like getting something they didn't expect. The effect can be magical. Endorsement letters can be long or short – whatever you need to get the job done. An endorsement letter can also be a 'lift-off' piece attached to the top of the endorsee's marketing materials.

Why should someone write an endorsement letter for you? Because the endorser gets their name in front of the prospect as they endorse you, and they may also reach new prospects from the endorsee's list. Also, the endorser benefits from creating the image of being a helpful entity.

THE FASTEST AND CHEAPEST WAY TO REACH THOUSANDS OF NEW CUSTOMERS IS THE PIGGY-BACK MAILING

Finally, the endorser does not necessarily have to be known to the recipient because the letter itself can serve to document the endorser's credentials, and explain why the letter is being written. This is another good way for both the endorser and endorsee to reach all new customers. In this latter case, both parties can share in cost of the mailing.

 Brainstorm 87

Coupons

It's next to impossible to suffer a loss when you employ a coupon strategy. Most often, using coupons means you make a nice profit. Studies show the average coupon issue pulls a 2-1 to 4-1 return on investment. The worst you can do is break even. Did you know that even lawyers, accountants, and those selling big-ticket items, like cars, almost always have tremendous results when using coupons? So why aren't you going to try a coupon right away, no matter what your business?

The best coupons are two-sided, use full colour, and larger coupons perform better than smaller sized ones. It's also a good idea to split-test them – that is, issue two different offers on two different coupons in a specified area and see which one does better. Now that you have a test, you can go with the best performer. A good coupon format is to print the front like an ad, and an advertorial on the back. Coupons also lend themselves to joint ventures. For example, every tenant in a professional building can print up an 11 x 17 sheet, each with their own coupon in the mix, and then pay to have the sheet inserted in a newspaper.

Coupons traditionally work best for food, fast food, dry cleaners, carpet cleaning and similar businesses, but as I said, they work almost as well for just about any kind of business, including professionals and big ticket items, from cars to kitchen appliances.

 Brainstorm 88

Sponsor community service

Doing charity work or sponsoring a community event is a powerful promotion and image building strategy. It's also a tremendous way to advertise. When you do good deeds, you create good feelings and good word-of-mouth advertising about your business. If you don't have a large budget, consider joint venture community service projects. Form a CIP – a Community Involvement Program with 10 or 20 other local businesses. You pool your resources and are able to do more.

Remember this: be selective about which projects you support. You want to support high visibility projects to get maximum exposure for your business. There's nothing wrong with being self serving while you do good work. The important thing is to do the good work! Also, look for projects that serve people who are most likely to be among your customer base, or your potential customer base.

Don't forget to sprinkle in some advertising where you can. For example, if you sponsor a 10-K run to raise funds for cancer research, give each runner a T-shirt with your logo on it.

Brainstorm 89

Catalogues

Selling with catalogues is high-powered selling. You have basically two options: print your own catalogues, or sell your products in someone else's catalogues. It's best to be the exclusive supplier of your product if you use other people's catalogues. Why? Because the catalogue owner can easily bypass you and go directly to your supplier and undercut you – unless you make an exclusive agreement not to allow that.

You can approach catalogue publishers on your own, or hire a catalogue broker.

There are two basic ways to make a deal with an existing catalogue to carry your product. First, you simply pay to have your product advertised in the catalogue. Second, you can offer your products at a discount to the catalogue and sell to them like a wholesaler. Some catalogues handle fulfilment for you, while others will send orders back to you for fulfilment. This is something you have to discuss with your catalogue host.

What about doing your own catalogue? Just about all major catalogue companies started out with a single product, and built its business from there. It can take years to build a customer base, a mailing list and a line of products numerous enough to fill an entire catalogue. Once you get to the level where you have enough items to fill a catalogue of several pages, you're already most likely making good money! Putting together a catalogue is more than just listing all your products – you need to write persuasive ad copy for each item you sell, you need photographs, layout, printers – and it's unlikely you can do all this yourself. That means hiring a variety of pros to handle all the special tasks, from copy writing to photography, and all the rest.

Once you have a catalogue of products to sell and a good mailing list, you're in serious business, making serious money. It's an exciting and challenging process when you start out with a single mail-order product, and build yourself into a full-blown catalogue company.

 Brainstorm 90

Contests

You can either create your own contest, or sponsor someone else's contest. Both are excellent marketing ideas. Let's talk about creating your own contest first. A contest will help you gather names and other vital marketing information about those who enter. A contest builds name recognition, enhances your company image, and provides excellent promotion opportunities, including free press.

Your contest must be designed around achieving sales and promotion goals, not just to have fun. Evaluate all your costs – what will you give away? How much will it cost to create contest details, such as contest forms, rules, advertising, distribution and more? Sending out a simple coupon people can fill out, mail in and get a chance to win is an easy way to gather a lot of new names. You can do this through direct mail, advertising, or you can try getting free ink by issuing a news release about your contest.

Another contest idea is a 'name the product' game. Invite the public to name your new product and give a prize to the winner. This can generate high public interest and score a lot of free press. Another idea is an 'essay contest.' Invite the public to write an essay about how your product changed their lives, or why your product is so good, etc. This can produce fantastic new marketing angles you may never have thought of before. The winning essay may be a highly inspirational story that you can use in future advertising, and which may end up getting good play in the media.

What about sponsoring someone else's contest? You have less control, but there's also less hassle. For example, a community fundraising drive to help build a library, park, or whatever, may seek prizes from local businesses to give away in exchange for fundraising activities. Donate your product, or money, and you'll get advertising benefits from the contest officials. If you are the sole sponsor, you may get your picture in the newspaper if you show up to give away your prize.

 Brainstorm 91

Prize draws

A prize draw is a simple kind of contest in which you invite people to submit their names, usually in a collection box set up in a store, for a chance to win something by random drawing. It's an excellent way to capture names and contact information, and other vital customer information for future selling. Make sure you get as much information as you can on the submission form. Go beyond name and phone number – get birthdays, ask for a product preference (make a simple check-off list) etc. Customers need to be present to win. Make the box prominent and easy to see. Offer an exciting prize to get a good response.

Brainstorm 92

Audio cassettes/CD ROMs/DVDs

I can't say enough about what fantastic marketing tools audio tapes and CDs are. They are classic 'long-copy' sales vehicles. That means you have a lot of time and space to make your best, full-blown sales pitch. Advertising on a free information-packed audio tape or CD in a small classified ad almost always produces fantastic response. If you make the tape or CD sound like it's a product of real value – in and of itself – that will tell the prospect something he or she badly wants to know, and they can get it free. You'll get dozens, hundreds, or even thousands of responses. Then you sit back and let the tape or CD do the selling for you! If you've packaged your sales material right, made a good offer, and salted your information with 'must order' information, you're going to make a lot of sales. Tapes and CDs are a bit more expensive to send out than paper-only sales material, but they work powerfully, and easily pay for themselves in the sales you generate. Once you have your information recorded, it costs very little, perhaps less than 50 pence each, to make copies of audio tapes and CDs, making them a dirt cheap way to sell to a lot of people with a very good, high-tech pitch.

TAPES AND CDS ARE A BIT MORE EXPENSIVE... BUT THEY WORK POWERFULLY, AND EASILY PAY FOR THEMSELVES IN THE SALES YOU GENERATE

Brainstorm 93

Video cassettes/CD ROMs/DVDs

A video-taped sales pitch is the next best thing to selling to a prospect face-to-face, and in some ways, even better than a live meeting with a customer. With video, you can dazzle your prospect with special effects, a 'live-on-tape' demonstration of the product and what it gets and does for the customer. A video tape is almost like cloning yourself, giving you the ability to meet face-to-face with thousands of clients all at once. Video tapes also carry a bit of that 'Wow!' factor; even today when video tapes are common in just about every household. The drawback to video is expense. The average professional video production rate these days is about £1,000 a minute. Don't even think of not having your video done by anyone but a pro. Your home video, no matter how good, just won't cut it. On the other hand, your video does not have to be very long. Even five minutes is a long time in the realm of video – it's more than long enough to make a full and complete pitch for your product.

Another good thing about video is the ease of transferring it to CD format, which can be played on most up-to-date home computers, or in home DVD players. A well produced CD or DVD has an even bigger 'Wow!' factor than video tape. Also, your DVD presentation can be played and accessed on the Internet, giving you the potential to reach many thousands of people every day.

Brainstorm 94

Magazine articles

A magazine article which puts your product or service in a favourable light is one of the most powerful selling tools known to man, or woman, for that matter. When was the last time you bought a magazine to read the ads? No, people buy magazines to read the articles. If an article gives good and positive information about your product, the response can be truly unbelievable. Readers will confront your product in a 'non-ad' environment, and thus their minds will be more open to all the positive information about your product. But how do you get a magazine to publish an article about your product? One way is to issue a press release to suggest an article, and hope a magazine reporter or editor agrees to write it. Another is to write an article yourself and submit it, or hire a free-lance writer to write it for you. As long as you remember that the purpose of the article is to serve the interests of the magazine's reader base, you have a shot at getting your article published. Make sure your article is not blatant advertising, but rather, a bona fide article with good information the readers can use. Mention your product only as an aside. Be subtle, but be sure to get your plug in. If you can slip in your 800-number, all the better. Getting a magazine article published is tough because most magazines get dozens of unsolicited submissions from freelance writers every day. Yet, hundreds of business men and women score a favourable magazine article somewhere just about every day. Stay at it. Keep submitting press releases and articles until you succeed. One other idea: get to know someone personally at the magazine, preferably an editor, and make your case for an article about your product when the time is right. With just the right charm, and just the right idea, you may get the publicity bonanza you've been searching for!

Brainstorm 95

Advertorials (long copy ads)

An advertorial can be 500% to 2,000% more responsive than a traditional ad. What is an advertorial and why do they work so well? An advertorial is an ad that looks more like a feature article in a newspaper or magazine. It uses the same type style as the host publication. It's written in news style, or in the writing style of the publication it appears in. An advertorial may also have a photo, and a headline. Most advertorials are designated as 'advertising' somewhere by the publications they run in. That's because the publication's editors have an obligation to tell their readers what's a paid ad, and what's a straight story. Never the less, the impact on the reader can be almost as good as if your advertorial were a real article. Advertorials must make an outright pitch for your product toward the end of the copy, however, and you must provide a clear way for the customer to contact you, or order. Writing an advertorial to look just right can be a bit of a challenge because it has to straddle that subtle line between regular news and advertising copy. Unless you have good writing skill, it's probably best to hire a pro to write your advertorial. But the power of the advertorial is that they look a lot less like an ad than a 'real' ad. The best advertising is that which does not look like advertising.

AN ADVERTORIAL CAN BE 500% TO 2,000% MORE RESPONSIVE THAN A TRADITIONAL AD.

Brainstorm 96

On-hold messages

The average person spends more than 60 hours per year on telephone hold! If you have to put people on hold, why waste time playing them some mindless muzak when you can use the time to deliver a sales message to them? If a person is willing to hold, you have their attention. And when you have attention, you're 80% of your way to a sale. Record a short advertising message to play and repeat during hold, and you'll make sales even while your employees are doing something else. The drawback is that you risk turning the caller off. The hang-up rate for hold is more than 80% – yet of those that do stay on hold, 85% listen to the entire message. Thus, you have little reason not to try this automated way to make more sales, especially if you're already putting people on hold anyway.

Also, be creative. A music shop used hold to play samples of newly released CDs. A bookstore used hold to read passages from new books. It's a great way to give customers a taste of something you would like them to buy.

Brainstorm 97

Business cards as ads

Your business card can and should do a lot more than simply announce who you are and where people can call you. They can do all the work of an ad, and do it very well.

Think of your business cards as a mobile, one-dimensional version of yourself. Put your picture on your card. It will help people associate your name with you and remember you because they can now picture you. Remember that your business card may the first impression people get of you and your company. You only get one chance to make a good first impression! A business card works to build your image, convey your personality, and is a solid and powerful reflection of you and your business.

Here are some business cards 'Dos'

- Make sure all your contact info is listed, including phone, fax, postal address and definitely your web page address.

- Include your picture and logo.

- Include your company motto, mission statement, or USP (Unique Selling Proposition).

- Use coloured stock or coloured ink.

- Put a discount coupon on the back of your card, or use the back to run an outright ad!

- List helpful information on the back of your card, such as emergency numbers, a calendar, helpful tips: this will give a reason for people to hold onto your card rather than toss it out at the first opportunity.

Some business Card 'Do Nots'

- Don't cross out outdated info by hand. Reprint new cards as soon as you need to change information.

- Don't go overboard with wild colours. No neon or glow-in-the-dark ink. Keep it light.

- Don't use fancy script fonts that are difficult to read.

- DON'T USE ALL CAPS.

- Don't use many different kinds of fonts.

- Don't make your design too busy or cluttered – don't try to do too much, while at the same time, develop a quick impact message that does more than just tell who you are.

 Brainstorm 98

Books

Writing and publishing your own book is a big project, but very worthwhile for the person who wants to achieve a whole new level of selling success. First, a book is a terrific positioning tool. If you write a book, you will be 'positioned' as an expert in your field. Second, a book can be a tool to sell more products, and advertise your business. For example, a used car dealer can write a book titled: *How to Get a Great Deal on a Used Car*. In the book, the author can refer readers to his web page, get them to call his freephone number, and of course, encourage them to come to his place of business in person. A book also lends itself to back-end sales. If people will buy a book, they may subscribe to a newsletter on a similar topic. List your newsletter at the back of the book, and you'll get subscribers. Now you have an additional vehicle to stay in contact with your customers, to advertise more of your products and keep the sales chain reaction going. If you're not a writer, or don't have time to write your own book, hire a ghost-writer. Doing so is a time-honoured tradition in the publishing world. A good ghost-writer will be able to write your book in about six weeks, depending on the length of your book. Ghost-writer fees vary widely, so shop around for a deal you can live with. You will most likely self publish your book. This has many advantages: you control all content, copyright, earnings and everything else. If your book sells well, you'll earn a lot of money while enjoying the positioning and marketing advantages afforded by your book.

Finally, a book is a marketing tool with a long shelf life. Your book can build your image and sell your products for years to come, so even if you put a lot of time, money and effort into getting your book published, it's almost always worth it.

 Brainstorm 99

Brochures

Everybody knows what a brochure is, but just about everybody makes poor use of them. Why? Because everybody makes the same mistakes. They forget that a brochure is supposed to sell something, and not merely show the product, and make the owner look good. Most brochures are printed with glossy paper, contain colour photographs and are filled with 'me oriented' copy. There's nothing especially wrong with glossy paper and photos, but the most important aspect of the brochure is to get prospects to take action: to come in, buy or both. Most brochures highlight features, rather than benefits. That's a critical mistake.

Common brochure mistakes are:

- Not having a strong headline to capture reader attention and draw them in.

- Not presenting information in super-easy-to-read format. Use more bullets, and fewer paragraphs of text.

- Forgetting testimonials.

- Using jargon and industry buzz words.

- Forgetting contact information.

- Not making an attractive offer.

- Using too many do-nothing photos.

- Using it as a self-bolstering ego enhancing tool.

Create your brochure with selling to customers in mind. Keep the focus on what the customer can expect to gain in all your brochure information. Include easy-to-find contact information, and even an order form. Include as many FAQ (frequently asked questions) as you can. The more questions you answer, the more blocks you remove to buying.

Brochures come in all sizes and shapes. The three-fold 'slim Jim' is the most common and popular. Use it if it fits your needs and budget, but don't be afraid to try a different format.

A brochure is another element of your overall marketing campaign. Don't duplicate information you already have in your sales letter or other marketing tools. But make it look consistent with all your other marketing tools. Your brochure must look like a member of your 'family,' bearing the same design elements and colour scheme. A brochure can build on what you say in your ads or sales letters. Remember, people must 'hear' or 'see' something from six to eight times before they actually absorb it. A brochure is one more way to hit the prospect in a way they will see, hear and act upon what you want them to act upon.

Brainstorm 100

Trade show booths

Trade shows are excellent venues for finding and selling more customers. If you set up a trade show booth, do so in a way designed to attract as many people as possible. It's not enough just to be present at a trade show. You have to put out some honey to attract the bees! That means an attention getting sign. It means offering something free – and that freebie has to be attractive enough to get people to stop and walk up to your booth. Once you get people to stop, have an arsenal of materials to hand out – including printed sales materials, audio and video brochures, and more. Don't forget your business card. Also, capture information! Entice people to fill out a survey, play a game, or register for a prize. The more information you get the better. This is an excellent way to build your all-important customer list, to which you can make future sales for months to come. Remember, the look of your booth says something about your company image. Make it look good!

Some final trade show tips

- Have the biggest sweet bowl in the place – and I mean the biggest- filled with colourful sweets!

- Get a media list, and make sure you invite every one of the media to come to your booth – then be ready to give them newsworthy information!

- Offer an exciting deal. Bring some products along and sell them at half price!

- Have a huge, lettered sign that easily attracts attention from a long way off.

- Follow-up on all trade show contacts within 24 hours! Doing so can increase sales an incredible 80%!

Brainstorm 101

Flea market stands

Having a stand at a flea market is similar to a trade show, though it may be less formal. Another drawback to a flea market is that the average customer may not be as highly qualified as those you find at a trade show. That's because trade shows tend to have a theme, while flea markets attract the general public, and mostly bargain hunters. Nevertheless, apply all of the tips you would at a normal trade show, and you'll have good results. Offer something free, have a big, easy-to-read sign that screams out an offer, and work the crowd with your bright personality to bring people to your stand. Be ready with sales materials and, don't forget to try to make sales right on the spot.

FOLLOW-UP ON ALL TRADE SHOW CONTACTS WITHIN 24 HOURS!

Brainstorm 102

Fairs

Fairs again are very similar to trade shows and flea markets, but with some differences. People go to fairs to have fun, not to conduct business. It only makes sense then to build some fun into your booth, and make it the primary attraction of your stand. At a trade show, everyone is focused on business first. At a fair, it's fun first. So when in Rome, do as the Romans do, but cleverly work in your marketing goals. Provide games of chance in exchange for customer information. Hand out free treats or helium balloons, along with brochures and marketing materials. Maybe you should dress like a clown! Hey, after all, it is a fair, and a clown will attract kids, and kids bring along their parents. Hand out free T-shirts and hats with your advertising messages imprinted on them. Collect as many names as possible, and don't forget to follow-up.

Brainstorm 103

MLM

Depending on who you talk to, MLM is either a scandalous dirty word, or an exciting pathway to riches. The word "scheme" and the term 'MLM' are often used together.

But to be objective, MLM doesn't have to be either. MLM – or Multi-Level Marketing – is basically the idea of getting others to sell for you in tiers. For example, if you hire five sales people to sell for

IN MY OPINION, THE VAST MAJORITY OF MLM OFFERINGS ARE SCAMS... IF THEY SOUND TOO GOOD TO BE TRUE, THEY PROBABLY ARE.

you, that's the first tier or level. Now, if each of those five people get five of their own sellers, that's the second level or tier – also known as a 'down-line' in MLM terms. The person on top of the first five sales people gets some of the earnings for the five under him – but also a cut from the five under each of his five. If the second tier five get sellers beneath them, the down-line gets bigger and bigger. At the top of the pyramid is the guy who started it all.

That's why MLM is often called a 'pyramid scheme.' It has made thousands of people rich over the past 50 years or so. Some of the most common MLM names are Amway and Shaklee. These companies have been pushing MLM arrangements for decades, and have continued to survive. Yet many other MLM distributors have been prosecuted for fraud.

The problem is that MLM models look good on paper, but as a matter of practicality, they don't work, and can't work. Thus the problem. One of the biggest criticisms of MLM is that everyone in the down-line must pay, or buy the products first before they can turn around and resell the products. Most of the time, it just doesn't work. The guy on the top of the pyramid always makes money because he is basically forcing his own sales people to buy from him, whether they sell something or not.

But what about MLM? Should you dabble in such an arrangement? Well, there is no reason why you can't set up a multi-level sales-force beneath you. The problem is that it's not as easy as you think. A successful MLM requires massive amounts of product, the right product, intense organizational skills, and much more.

You may be better off using certain aspects of MLM, rather than developing a classic pyramid scheme. For example, I have a business colleague who sells a turn-key home publishing package. His customers get 12 issues of a newsletter, a video and a 50-page booklet, and reprint rights to sell all of the above. They pay £300 for the reprint rights.

But my colleague benefits in pyramid fashion from his package because the newsletters he supplies to his buyers are sprinkled with advertising for his own products. Thus, his customers pay him £300 to go out and sell his newsletters, which in turn bring him more customers by getting his ads spread out for free. It has some aspects of MLM in that his buyers help him promote his business further, and the more they sell, the more prospects he reaches. It's different from a classic pyramid strategy in that the end users do not become part of a classic down-line.

Use your own judgment on MLM. In my opinion, the vast majority of MLM offerings are scams. If they sound too good to be true, they probably are. But you can still build some MLM aspects into your own selling efforts, and you can get very rich fast if it works for you.

Brainstorm 104

Surveys

Why does a seller need to conduct surveys? Because the true key to selling is knowing everything you can about each prospect. The more you know, the easier it is to sell. It's that simple. A survey is also a way to sell. Let's say you call a 1,000 people and conduct a quick customer survey. You're not selling at this point, merely gathering information. You may offer a gift to thank the prospect for taking part in your survey. The next time you call, it's not going to be a cold call. The prospect knows you, and you know a lot about the prospect, including their needs and wants, so you can fulfil those needs and wants, and make sales. You can conduct surveys from a public booth, at trade shows, by using a contest or prize drawing. You can mail a survey and offer a free gift to all who respond. Those who do respond will be very hot prospects. Now you've got a good customer list to send your direct marketing materials to. Some of the big companies hire marketing research firms to conduct surveys to determine the lay of the land – that is, if a particular geographic area is ripe for what the company sells. It's expensive, but it pays off because the company is no longer selling blind. They're not wasting their precious marketing budget on an area that is not likely to yield sales. You don't have to hire pros to do your surveys. You can design and administer your own. You can also hold workshops and focus groups – great ways to learn customer information, and build your selling list at the same time. Do your own surveys on whatever level you can afford. It won't be a waste of time, and you'll find new customer sources you may never have discovered otherwise.

Brainstorm 105

TV talk shows

Getting yourself invited as a guest on a TV talk show is a terrific free advertising/promotion strategy. You position yourself as an expert in your field, and you get to plug your product to an attentive TV audience. The trick is to get invited. Why would anyone consider you as a potential TV guest? If you:

- Fill an audience need.
- Have a solution to a common problem.
- Are entertaining.
- Have newsworthy information.
- Appeal to the TV target audience.

You can help your chances by publishing a book in your area of expertise. You can also write a column. You can also list yourself in professional directories, where TV producers often look for guests.

Watch TV shows you think you have a chance at, and monitor their content and format. Once you understand what the show is about and what they need, you can meet that need. Send a press release or a media package to the station manager and suggest yourself as a guest. Include a photo of yourself and list your areas of speciality.

If you get on the show, make sure to tape it, and use it in your future marketing efforts. Also get a transcript and publish it in your newsletter. Make sure you tell the local newspaper that you're going to be on TV. Make sure you bring along your 0800-number and give it while you're on the show.

Brainstorm 106

Newsletters

If you're not publishing your own newsletter, start planning one today. A newsletter is a high-powered selling and customer relations tool. It's also a way to get free media – and you can even make money by selling advertising in it to others.

And get this: studies show that newsletters have a 400% higher readership rate than any other kind of direct mail you can send to your customers. That in itself is enough to develop and distribute a newsletter.

A newsletter helps you build name recognition. A newsletter builds your credibility and bolsters your image as an expert in your field. Newsletters generate repeat sales. Newsletters keep your customers informed about your company, tells them what's new, and how they can get great deals others can't. Your newsletter can be a prime tool to build a preferred customer list.

Newsletters can be hard sell or soft sell. The first kind is heavily tilted toward getting customers to buy. It's filled with product endorsements, hard-hitting sales copy, photos of your products, reasons to buy, etc. A soft sell goes lighter on the selling and concentrates more on promotion, educating your customers, and building your image.

Hard sell newsletters bare the risk of turning customers off, while soft sell newsletters bear the risk of not doing enough to help your bottom line. You'll have to test your newsletter carefully to strike the right balance.

A NEWSLETTER IS A HIGH-POWERED SELLING AND CUSTOMER RELATIONS TOOL.

Perhaps the biggest drawback of a newsletter is the time it takes to put it together. Never forget: publishing even a small newsletter can be extremely challenging and time consuming. It needs to be written, designed, laid out, printed, mailed: all tasks someone in your organization must do. You can always farm the job out to a professional, but it's likely to cost plenty. Still, a newsletter done right is almost always worth the effort and cost in what it will do for your sales and company image.

 Brainstorm 107

Correspondence course

I know a person who is an expert in creativity, and specifically, in using dreams to promote creativity. He has a degree in psychology, but his real passion is selling. Using his knowledge of the dreaming mind, and learning theory, my friend put together a course called 'Stimulating Creativity with Dreams.'

After having some success conducting workshops and teaching some night classes, my friend decided to package his idea as a correspondence course. He advertised it on the World Wide Web, and soon was signing up dozens of participants per month. He charged a modest fee for the course, which was totally conducted over the web, but he really cleaned up in selling a three-ring binder Dream Creativity Home Study Course which expanded on the correspondence course. It included an audio tape and other items. He sold the package for £108 each, and within months, was selling more than 50 a month – which is £5,400 a month! Not bad for a guy who never has to leave his house, and who does no direct selling!

If you sell wine, why not set up a wine tasting correspondence course, and sell wine to your students? If you're an auto mechanic, create a study program for basic car care – and then sell care products.

A correspondence course is a terrific way to attract people who want to gain knowledge, and who will pay you to get it – and they'll buy any other product you care to sell on the back end!

 Brainstorm 108

Personal sales contacts

Selling face-to-face is real selling. It may also be the most difficult kind of selling to master. If you can't deal with rejection, you'll never make it in personal sales. But those who can learn to accept rejection as an opportunity for learning, and who master the art of personal selling, have the world at their fingertips. When you master personal selling, nothing can stop you from selling your way to all the money and free time you could ever want.

Here are my Top 10 Tips for Mastering Personal Sales Calls

1. Be goal oriented: remember that goals fill needs. Choose your goals carefully. What are your needs? Answer that question first and then set your goals to fill those needs. Good selling starts with yourself, and what you want to accomplish.

2. Use self-management techniques: a great sales person has to be a self-starter. Make wise use of your time and talents.

3. Never procrastinate: do the things you hate first and get them behind you quickly.

4. Be unflinchingly positive: remember that 'No' means 'Maybe' and 'Maybe' means 'Yes.'

5. Take a genuine interest in your customer, suppliers, and co-workers: don't fake it. Live it!

6. Ask questions and listen: how can you fulfil your customers' needs or solve their problems if you don't ask them what they are? Very often you'll find out that what you thought you knew was the opposite of the truth!

7. Make personal contact: letters and e-mail are fine for making appointments, but face-to-face contact is still the strongest way to make sales and build a relationship.

8. Be honest, keep your promises: always do what you say you're going to do. Deliver more than you promise.

9. Never stop learning: keep reading books just like this one! Find others as well. Follow selling courses and find a mentor. Learn directly from a pro. You can never know it all, but the more knowledge you gain, the stronger your sales skills get.

10. Enjoy and be passionate about selling: if you're not having a terrific time, you're wasting your time. This is probably more true of sales than anything else.

Brainstorm 109

Party plans

More than a billion dollars of merchandise is sold every year via the in-home party. I can think of five companies that have earned enormous profits with this kind of marketing strategy: TupperWare, Amway and Avon, Virgin Cosmetics and more recently Pampered Chef. It works this way: the seller invites a number of guests to his or her home for a combination social gathering/selling event. The host provides food, drinks and activities, one of which is showing a line or products for guests to purchase. The host can either have the product on site ready to buy, or have samples and catalogues which guests peruse and make orders from if they want.

This is a marketing strategy that works well for some, but not for others. For example, a person who becomes a Tupperware dealer will most likely invite friends, family and acquaintances to their first selling party. But after all the people they know have been exhausted, they need to take the party process a step further by finding new party guests, including people they don't know. That's where it gets difficult for most, and that's where most drop out and try something else.

But the key in keeping the process going is finding people who come to your first one or two parties to agree to be the next hosts – and they in turn invite additional people the original seller may not know personally. The selling point is that the next person to hold a party gets a cut of the next round of sales. The process continues this way, going from party to party, each time enlisting a fresh host.

The bad rap on selling parties is that some people think they're in bad taste. Many feel it's tacky to invite friends and family over, only to sell them stuff.

I think it's all a matter of perspective and the way in which the host approaches this kind of sales strategy. The key is in being upfront with people. You don't want to 'ambush' your guests. That is, don't invite people over for what they think is going to be a pure social event, and then spring a line of products upon them and pressure them into making a purchase. Rather, let them know from the beginning that this is going to be an occasion to view and sample products that they may be interested in, and that they can get terrific bargains on items that will be of good use and practicality for them. At the same time, there'll be some fun, socializing, food, and simply a chance to have a nice time. Make it known that no one is under any obligation to buy, and that there will definitely be no hard sell. The key is getting people to come, have a good time, and let the products sell themselves. Fortunately, that usually happens. Once you get the horse to water, so to speak, they'll drink once they learn how the product can be something worth owning, how they can save money over buying the product off the shelf somewhere, and how they may even earn their money back plus more if they host the next party.

MORE THAN A BILLION DOLLARS OF MERCHANDISE IS SOLD EVERY YEAR VIA THE IN-HOME PARTY.

This kind of selling requires a certain finesse on behalf of the seller. A gifted in-home entertainer and 'people person' will find party selling a terrific way to find a lot of new clients, and sell to them in an environment that is casual and fun. The other key is to keep the 'chain reaction' of parties going. Some party sellers get more ambitious and hold very large events at hotels, and may invite dozens or even hundreds of 'guests.' Such an event can generate thousands of pounds in sales in a single afternoon.

I encourage anyone to give this selling strategy a try. It's a proven selling system – if you're the right person to make it work.

 Brainstorm 110

Interviews on audio/video

An excellent way to promote yourself or your business is to stage an interview on video or audio tape. For example, let's say Bob Johnson is a successful antiques dealer and trader, and let's say a business reporter wants to sit Bob down for a discussion of the rare antiques industry. In the course of the interview, the reporter covers a wide range of topics, including what it takes to be a success in this field. If Bob gives insightful answers to the reporter's questions, what you have is an excellent and informative presentation that others interested in rare antiques can learn from. It can also attract new customers because those who see or hear the interview will come to view Bob as an expert in his field, and they'll be eager to do business with him – because he's one of the best.

You can stage your own interviews and put them on audio or video tape. You don't need to wait for a reporter to take notice of you and call you for an interview. Simply hire someone to take the role of interviewer, provide a script and do the interview. The questions can be scripted, but your answers don't have to be – you simply talk about your business because you already know it best – though you should plan specific points to cover, including giving reasons for others to do business with you.

The interview format is a pleasant and informative way to distribute information about what you do, build your image as an expert, and attract new customers. Once your interview is on tape, you have a superb selling tool which you can distribute in any number of ways, from direct mail to live distribution.

 Brainstorm 111

Association memberships

Just about every industry I can think of has a professional association. Whether you sell clothing, lumber or toys, you can bet there's trade or professional organization where all can meet once or several times a year to exchange ideas, brainstorm new strategies, talk about industry trends, and more.

You can take advantage of these groups in two ways. First, become a member. You'll benefit from sharing ideas with your fellow sellers in your field, and you'll find ways to improve your own lot. Second, professional associations are excellent ways to find your ideal target market. For example, if you sell haulage equipment, such as truck trailers, you'll find plenty of new prospects at a trucker's association convention. Attend their meetings and conventions, or even get yourself invited as a speaker. While there, network aggressively. Meet people, make friends and connections. Ask your new friends who they think might need your product, and you'll get plenty of leads. When you sell to one person, bring along a list of names of fellow association members and ask your new customer, "Bob, who else on this list do you think might need what I'm selling?" As Bob will know many of the names on your list, you'll get some hot leads. Better still, when you meet with the new prospect, you can tell them "Bob sent you." This is just an excellent, sometimes even effortless, way to sell.

 Brainstorm 112

Conferences

Let's say a company sells medical supplies. Such a company can put on a conference for nurses entitled, 'New Challenges in Infection Prevention.' The conference may count as a continuing education credit, which all nurses must continue to obtain throughout their careers. The company can charge a fee for attendance, a fee which is most often paid for by the employer. Let's say 200 nurses attend the conference. In addition to supplying the educational content, the company can also pitch its products to nurses and make a lot of sales.

Now let's say Bob Jones sells medical malpractice insurance for nurses. Bob hears about the conference and gets himself invited to the conference as a featured speaker, or maybe he sets up a table in the lobby at the hotel where the convention is being held. There he'll find a lot of new leads, and he'll make a lot of sales if he plays his cards right.

The conference strategy can work for just about any kind of business. A company that sells pet grooming supplies can put on a conference for professional dog groomers called, 'Winning Dog Show Strategies.' When the attendees arrive, they have a captive audience to move more of their products, while providing an educational forum for professional self improvement.

A conference can be a double barrelled selling strategy – prospects pay to attend, and they make purchases while they're there. That's the kind of selling situation any seller can live with, and live well!

Conclusion

Now The Work Really Begins!

Well done for making it through to the end of this book. But of course it isn't really the end because now your real journey begins. It's time for you to start putting these powerful and effective methods, strategies and techniques into practice in your business. Don't delay, don't hesitate, don't procrastinate. Do it now!

You know that just reading about these concepts isn't going to do you any good whatsoever. You've got to do something with them! That means action!

One effective way of taking action is to develop a plan. We spoke about planning right at the beginning in Chapter 1. In putting together your plan make sure that you use a range of strategies to build your business. It's just common sense that if you are using a plethora of profit generating strategies then if one or two fall short, you'll have the benefit of the rest to boost your bottom-line. Furthermore, by doing this you boost your chance of success and exponentially increase the results.

I've thoroughly enjoyed this exploration with you into business building. I hope I've succeeded in providing you with the insights, the tools and the methodology to help you to literally skyrocket your business!

Feel free to contact me or one of my Quantum team if you feel that you need help or you would like to implement the methods contained in this book but just don't have the time or energy. We'd be delighted to help.

By the way, there's some special offers for you to take advantage of in the following few pages… Hey, I practice what I preach!

All the very best, and may I wish you every success!

David Abingdon
david@davidabingdon.com

FREE Subscription To David Abingdon's 'Business Growth Strategies' Newsletter

Yes, you can now receive absolutely free one of the most exciting, thought provoking and profit producing business newsletters you will ever read.

Why? Because revealed in these pages you are going to find an abundance of no-nonsense, power-packed and wealth building features of real substance for you to implement immediately into your daily business activities.

With 'Business Growth Strategies', you are going to be armed to the teeth with an arsenal of powerful sales and marketing weapons to literally 'explode' your business growth and propel your profits to levels that you never thought possible. You will gain an unfair advantage that will leave your competitors - whatever their size - scampering for cover and wondering what it was that hit them.

Every article and report is written in a clear, concise and practical manner to present you with proven and beneficial business building ideas, tips, strategies, secrets, techniques, methods, concepts, principles, tactics, real life examples and, most of all, cutting edge tools.

'Business Growth Strategies' will slash years off your business and personal goals by literally forcing you down the fast-track to success.

Utilize, Profit and Enjoy!

Mail to: FREE Newsletter Offer,
The Quantum Organization, Quantum House,
Bonds Mill, Stonehouse, Gloucestershire GL10 3RF, UK
or
The Quantum Organization, Level 17, 201 Miller Street,
North Sydney 2060, AUSTRALIA

Or Fax: UK: 01453 794811 • Outside UK: + 44 1453 794810
AUSTRALIA: 02 9959 2244 • Outside AUS: + 61 2 9959 2244

Or Email: bookoffer@QuantumOrg.com
Please type: 'Free Newsletter Offer' in the subject line.

David Abingdon's FREE Newsletter Offer

YES, please send me your invaluable Business Growth
Strategies newsletter.

Name _____

Company _____

Address _____

_____

_____

_____

Postcode/Zip_____Country _____

Email _____

Telephone _____

Visit David's website at: www.DavidAbingdon.com

Take Advantage Of David's FREE Business Assessment Offer

"Get All The Tools, Strategies And Systems YOU Need To Give You A Formidable And Unfair Advantage In The Marketplace".

You can now have one of David Abingdon's licensed Quantum Business Development Consultant's to help you to take your business to the next level...

You'll find out how a Quantum Business Development Consultant uses proven, no cost and low cost methods to help you:

- Drive hordes of hungry customers to your business.

- Craft and use powerful and irresistible marketing strategies to drive your sales through the roof.

- Counter competitor price cutting without reducing your margins.

- Uncover and profit from the hidden assets to be found in your business.

- Quickly, simply and effectively increase sales to your current customers by 10%, 35% and even 90%, with no additional marketing costs.

- Find, acquire, keep and motivate superstar salespeople and employees.

- Live and enjoy greater success by rapidly building a highly profitable business that will run itself.

- Get and use testimonials to dramatically boost your sales.

- Double, triple even quadruple your sales conversion rate.

- Make your business 100% recession proof in 30 days or less.

And much, much more…

Just mail the coupon to Quantum for a FREE business development assessment and you could be well on your way to achieving the business success you always dreamed of:

David Abingdon's FREE Business Assessment Offer

YES, please send me details of your FREE Business Assessment Offer.

Name _____

Company_____

Address _____

_____

_____

_____

Postcode/Zip_____Country _____

Email _____

Telephone _____

Mail to: FREE Newsletter Offer,
The Quantum Organization, Quantum House,
Bonds Mill, Stonehouse, Gloucestershire GL10 3RF, UK
or
The Quantum Organization, Level 17,
201 Miller Street, North Sydney 2060,
AUSTRALIA

Or Fax: UK: 01453 794811 • Outside UK: + 44 1453 794810
AUSTRALIA: 02 9959 2244 • Outside AUS: + 61 2 9959 2244

Or Email: bookoffer@QuantumOrg.com
Please type: 'Free Newsletter Offer' in the subject line.

Visit David's website at: www.DavidAbingdon.com

Other titles from Thorogood

GURUS ON MARKETING

Sultan Kermally

£14.99 paperback, ISBN 1 85418 243 9
£24.99 hardback, ISBN 1 85418 238 2
Published November 2003

Kermally has worked directly with many of the figures in this book, including Peter Drucker, Philip Kotler and Michael Porter. It has enabled him to summarise, contrast and comment on the key concepts with knowledge, depth and insight, and to offer you fresh ideas to improve your own business. He describes the key ideas of each 'guru', places them in context and explains their significance. He shows you how they were applied in practice, looks at their pros and cons and includes the views of other expert writers.

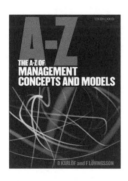

THE A-Z OF MANAGEMENT CONCEPTS AND MODELS

B. Karlöf and F. Lövingsson

£18.99 paperback, ISBN 1 85418 390 7
£35.00 hardback, ISBN 1 85418 385 0
Published May 2005

An A to Z of all the essential concepts and models applied in business and management, from Balanced scorecard and the Boston matrix to Experience curve, Kaizen, McKinsey's 7S model, Market analysis, Porter's generic strategies, Relative cost position, Sustainable development to Yield management and Zero-based planning.

THE A-Z OF EMPLOYMENT PRACTICE

David Martin

£19.99 paperback, ISBN 1 85418 380 X
£42.00 hardback, ISBN 1 85418 300 1
Published November 2004

This book provides comprehensive, practical guidance on personnel law and practice at a time when employers are faced with a maze of legislation, obligations and potential penalties. It provides detailed and practical advice on what to do and how to do it.

The A to Z format ensures that sections appear under individual headings for instant ease of reference. The emphasis is not so much on the law as on its implications; the advice is expert, clear and practical, with a minimum of legal references. Checklists, procedures and examples are all given as well as warnings on specific pitfalls.

MARKETING STRATEGY DESKTOP GUIDE

Norton Paley

£16.99 paperback, ISBN 1 85418 139 4
Published 2000

A practical source of reference, guidance, techniques and best practice, with an abundance of summaries, checklists, charts and special tips. Contents include: market segmentation; marketing strategy; competitive position; market research; customer behaviour; products and services; pricing; promotion mix; sales force; marketing plan; financial tools of marketing.

"A remarkable resource...indispensable for the Marketing Professional" DAVID LEVINE, V-P STRATEGIC SOURCING, NABS INC, USA

MASTERING MARKETING
The core skills of profitable
marketing
Ian Ruskin-Brown

£14.99 paperback, ISBN 1 85418 123 8
£22.00 hardback, ISBN 1 85418 118 1
Published 1999

An understanding of the key principles and techniques of marketing is vital for managers of all levels, and not just those in the marketing department. This book gives clear guidance on the skills and concepts required to market your business profitably. It will prove invaluable to those wishing to adopt a more structured approach to business developent.

SUCCESSFUL SELLING SOLUTIONS
Test, monitor and constantly improve
your selling skills
Julian Clay

£12.99 paperback, ISBN 1 85418 242 0
£22.50 hardback, ISBN 1 85418 298 6
Published September 2003

This book is like having a personal coach at your side. Using self-assessment models it shows you how to track your progress in your sales campaigns, how to identify where you may be going wrong and how to build a successful sales path of development. It provides a variety of templates, tables, exercises and ideas alongside clear, practical advice on every aspect of making a sale.

"Julian Clay is a master of the selling process..."
LAWRIE SITEMAN, MANAGING DIRECTOR, IDS GROUP

SUCCESSFUL BUSINESS PLANNING

Norton Paley

£14.99 paperback, ISBN 1 85418 277 3
£29.99 hardback, ISBN 1 85418 289 7
Published June 2004

We know the value of planning – in theory. But either we fail to spend the time required to go through the thinking process properly, or we fail to use the plan effectively. Paley uses examples from real companies to turn theory into practice.

"Growth firms with a written business plan have increased their revenues 69 per cent faster over the past five years than those without a written plan."

FROM A SURVEY BY PRICEWATERHOUSECOOPERS

WIN NEW BUSINESS – THE DESKTOP GUIDE

Susan Croft

£16.99 paperback, ISBN 1 85418 290 0,
Published November 2002

Packed with innovative ways of generating leads, here is a practical source of advice and techniques for winning new business from both new and existing customers. It provides the essential skills for: analysing customer needs and building relationships; understanding the psychology of selling; writing successful proposals and making outstanding presentations; pushing through to win.

"... packed with useful information and should be essential reading for anyone in business development".

GLORIA VERGARI, CHIEF EXECUTIVE OFFICER,
NORSTAR BIOMAGNETICS LTD UK

BUSINESS SEMINARS

Focused on developing your potential

Falconbury, the sister company to Thorogood publishing, brings together the leading experts from all areas of management and strategic development to provide you with a comprehensive portfolio of action-centred training and learning.

We understand everything managers and leaders need to be, know and do to succeed in today's commercial environment. Each product addresses a different technical or personal development need that will encourage growth and increase your potential for success.

- Practical public training programmes
- Tailored in-company training
- Coaching
- Mentoring
- Topical business seminars
- Trainer bureau/bank
- Adair Leadership Foundation

The most valuable resource in any organization is its people; it is essential that you invest in the development of your management and leadership skills to ensure your team fulfil their potential. Investment into both personal and professional development has been proven to provide an outstanding ROI through increased productivity in both you and your team. Ultimately leading to a dramatic impact on the bottom line.

With this in mind Falconbury have developed a comprehensive port-folio of training programmes to enable managers of all levels to develop their skills in leadership, communications, finance, people management, change management and all areas vital to achieving success in today's commercial environment.

What Falconbury can offer you?

- Practical applied methodology with a proven results
- Extensive bank of experienced trainers
- Limited attendees to ensure one-to-one guidance
- Up to the minute thinking on management and leadership techniques
- Interactive training
- Balanced mix of theoretical and practical learning
- Learner-centred training
- Excellent cost/quality ratio

Falconbury In-Company Training

Falconbury are aware that a public programme may not be the solution to leadership and management issues arising in your firm. Involving only attendees from your organization and tailoring the programme to focus on the current challenges you face individually and as a business may be more appropriate. With this in mind we have brought together our most motivated and forward thinking trainers to deliver tailored in-company programmes developed specifically around the needs within your organization.

All our trainers have a practical commercial background and highly refined people skills. During the course of the programme they act as facilitator, trainer and mentor, adapting their style to ensure that each individual benefits equally from their knowledge to develop new skills.

Falconbury works with each organization to develop a programme of training that fits your needs.

Mentoring and coaching

Developing and achieving your personal objectives in the workplace is becoming increasingly difficult in today's constantly changing environment. Additionally, as a manager or leader, you are responsible for guiding colleagues towards the realization of their goals. Sometimes it is easy to lose focus on your short and long-term aims.

Falconbury's one-to-one coaching draws out individual potential by raising self-awareness and understanding, facilitating the learning and performance development that creates excellent managers and leaders. It builds renewed self-confidence and a strong sense of 'can-do' competence, contributing significant benefit to the organization. Enabling you to focus your energy on developing your potential and that of your colleagues.

Mentoring involves formulating winning strategies, setting goals, monitoring achievements and motivating the whole team whilst achieving a much improved work life balance.

Falconbury – Business Legal Seminars

Falconbury Business Legal Seminars specialises in the provision of high quality training for legal professionals from both in-house and private practice internationally.

The focus of these events is to provide comprehensive and practical training on current international legal thinking and practice in a clear and informative format.

Event subjects include, drafting commercial agreements, employment law, competition law, intellectual property, managing an in-house legal department and international acquisitions.

For more information on all our services please contact: Falconbury on +44 (0)20 7729 6677 or visit the website at: www.falconbury.co.uk.